HANDS ON

Crafts for Kids®

20-Minute Crafts

HANDS ON

Crafts for Kids®

20-Minute Crafts

Sterling Publishing Co., Inc.
New York
A Sterling / Chapelle Book

Chapelle:

Jo Packham, Owner

Cathy Sexton, Editor

Staff: Areta Bingham, Kass Burchett, Marilyn Goff, Holly Hollingsworth, Susan Jorgensen,
Barbara Milburn, Linda Orton, Karmen Quinney, Cindy Stoeckl, Kim Taylor,
Sara Toliver, Kristi Torsak

Photography: Kevin Dilley for Hazen Imaging, Inc., and Scot Zimmerman

If you have any questions or comments or would like information on specialty products
featured in this book, please contact Chapelle, Ltd., Inc., P.O. Box 9252, Ogden, UT 84409
(801) 621-2777 • (801) 621-2788 Fax • e-mail: chapelle@chapelleltd.com •
website: www.chapelleltd.com

Library of Congress Cataloging-in-Publication Data Available

10 9 8 7 6 5 4 3 2 1

Published by Sterling Publishing Company, Inc.
387 Park Avenue South, New York, NY 10016
© 2001 by Hands On Crafts for Kids
Distributed in Canada by Sterling Publishing
c/o Canadian Manda Group, One Atlantic Avenue, Suite 105
Toronto, Ontario, Canada M6K 3E7
Distributed in Great Britain and Europe by Chris Lloyd at Orca Book
Services, Stanley House, Fleets Lane, Poole BH15 3AJ, England
Distributed in Australia by Capricorn Link (Australia) Pty. Ltd.
P.O. Box 704, Windsor, NSW 2756, Australia
Printed in the USA
All Rights Reserved

Sterling ISBN 0-8069-2517-5

about the author

kathie
stull

*The
Hands On
theme:
"All
kids
are
creative!"*

The creation of Hands On Crafts for Kids® by Kathie Stull is the result of a varied background, spanning over 24 years in the craft industry. A degree in marketing and design led her to the how-to industry—first as a buyer, and then to forming her own company representing print media in the craft industry. She also conducted seminars and workshops for both kids and adults.

Print advertising led to the development of other mediums including television. Kathie is the marketing agent for some of the best known how-to programs on public television, including: America Sews, Quilting from the Heartland, and Sew Young Sew Fun. She also produces the television programs: More Than Memories, The NeedleArts Studio with Shay Pendray and, of course, Hands On Crafts for Kids.

This book is the sixth title in the Hands On series. The theme: "All kids are creative!" is found throughout the Hands On books, television programs, related products, and web site. Hands On is seen nationally on public television, internationally in many countries, and is used for curriculum in 19 states. The Hands On programs are founded on the premise of providing fun and educational activities for children. Crafts are seen not only as an activity, but as a way to build self-esteem and develop the creative spirit found in ALL children.

A mother of three, Kathie uses this experience in developing meaningful projects for children. She is a former board member of the Association of Craft and Creative Industries, Chair of National Craft Month, and current board member of Adventures in the Arts—a program to bring arts and crafts to inner-city children.

table of contents

introduction

Artwork by Daniel Savage

If you've got 20 minutes, we'll help you be creative!

This new book from Hands On Crafts for Kids is all about having fun while making craft projects, even when you only have a little time.

The Hands On philosophy: "There is no right or wrong way to craft!"

This book is filled with quick ideas for creative crafting for family and friends. We provide fun, educational projects for kids 7 to 12 years of age—and, of course, their parents, group leaders, and/or care providers. Keep in mind the Hands On theme: "All kids are creative!" and the Hands On philosophy: "There is no right or wrong way to craft!"

We want to encourage you to substitute your favorite colors and add supplies that you have around the house. Adding your own special details will make the projects reflect you.

The concept of Hands On Crafts for Kids was originally developed to address the need for activities for kids. In a high-tech society, there is still the need for "high-touch" alternatives. Kids at home can have fun crafting while actually reinforcing some of the concepts they may learn at school. Teachers can use Hands On as a supplement to their teaching of academic subjects.

A hands-on activity can increase the self-esteem of a child and allow for the development of their natural talents.

This latest addition to the Hands On library continues with the Hands On concept providing projects that are quick, easy, and inexpensive! The projects were developed by the leading designers in the craft industry in a simple and easy-to-follow format. The projects feature full-sized patterns and easy-to-find supplies.

All you need is 20 minutes to discover the creativity in you!

three important elements

Artwork by Rebecca Hendricks

1
creativity

Crafting is a wonderful way for children to express themselves and build self-esteem. The projects are designed to encourage development of individual style and expression in kids.

2
crafting with a purpose

The Hands On television program often profiles kids who are helping other kids through their crafts. We invite you to help your children and students explore ways to use their crafting to help others. It may be as simple as making a card for a senior citizen, or maybe making more than one of a particular project and selling them to raise money for charity.

A portion of the profits generated from Hands On is used to provide kids the opportunity to be creative.

3
knowledge

Learning takes place through well-designed, curriculum-based creative projects. As kids explore their creativity, they will also learn basic skills such as measuring, cutting, symmetry, balance, and color theory.

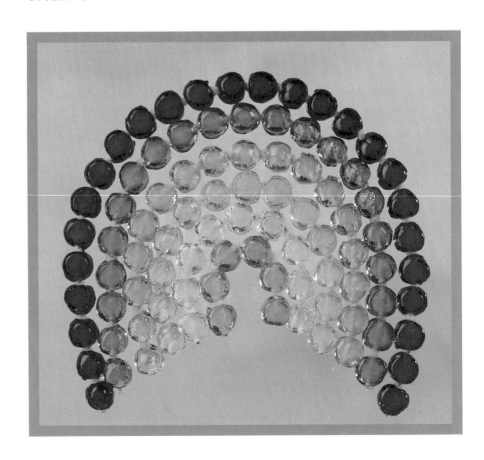

before you begin

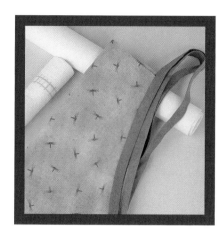

preparing your work surface

It is important to prepare your work surface by covering it with newspaper, butcher paper, or a drop cloth. If spills of any kind occur, your work surface will be protected. Remember to keep a roll of paper towels handy to wipe up spills.

protecting your clothing

It is always a good idea to wear play clothes when doing crafts of any kind. Even then, wearing an apron or an old shirt is a great idea.

learning how to read dimensions

Dimensions are the width and length or height of an object. When a specific dimension is called for in a materials list, it will be written with an "x" meaning "by"—such as 6" wide x 12" long. Don't confuse this "x" for the multiplication or times symbol.

In addition, some abbreviations are used— such as dia. for the word diameter. If there are abbreviations that you are not familiar with, just ask any adult.

transferring patterns

The patterns in this book have been printed at actual size. If you want to make them larger or smaller, you will need to use a copy machine to enlarge or reduce the patterns accordingly.

To transfer the pattern, first you need to trace the pattern with a pencil from the book onto tracing paper. Cut out the traced pattern, then draw around it on the material you will be working with—soft-foam sheeting, card stock, felt, etc.

Another way to transfer patterns that have been traced onto tracing paper is to turn the traced pattern over, placing the "pencil" side to the material you will be working with. On the back side of the tracing paper, trace over the lines again with the pencil. This will very lightly transfer the pencil lines onto the material.

choosing a paintbrush

There are many different types of paintbrushes available—with bristles made from synthetic fibers to bristles made from natural fibers. Paintbrush bristles also come in different shapes and sizes—such as round and flat. When choosing a paintbrush for a specific project, the best factor for determining the size you need will be the size of the project or area of the project to be painted. If the project is a large one, you will want a large paintbrush —like a 2" flat-bristle. If the project is a small one, you will want a small paintbrush—like a $1/4$" flat-bristle. Foam brushes are also available and are easy to use.

painting basics

Once you have chosen a paintbrush that is appropriately sized for the project you are going to paint, you will want to keep a few things in mind while you are painting. Remember to paint all surfaces of the project. For example, if you are painting a wooden shape, you need to paint the sides and/or edges of the wood, in addition to the flat, top surface.

If the first coat of paint seems a little thin, don't hesitate to add a second coat. Just remember to let the paint thoroughly dry between coats and before moving on to the next step.

The paints that have been called for in this book are acrylic paints. There is an amazing number of paint colors available and these paints are water-based so they clean up easily.

For each project in this book that requires a paintbrush, all you will need is one. However, it is important to rinse the paintbrush before using a new paint color. If you prefer, a separate paintbrush can be used for each color.

If you choose to seal the painted project, a sealer that is suitable for use with acrylic paints should be brushed on. If your project has been made to be displayed outside, you will definitely want to seal the paint to keep it from cracking and chipping.

dry-brushing

This painting technique is done with a dry paintbrush. Simply load the paintbrush with a small amount of paint, brush it over a paper towel to remove excess

paint, then brush the project in a scrubbing motion to apply the paint.

adding dots and highlights

Once in a while you will need to paint dots or highlights. For example, cheeks are often made with a single dot on each side of a face. Sometimes, dots are used as accents.

Dots and highlights are easily painted by loading the end of a paintbrush handle with paint, then applying it to your project. It is important to lift the paintbrush handle straight up from the project after applying the dot or the paint could smear. Repeat the process for each dot

needed. Wipe off the end of the paintbrush handle as often as necessary to keep the dots uniform in size.

Cotton swabs can also be used for this purpose, but will need to be replaced as the cotton becomes saturated with paint.

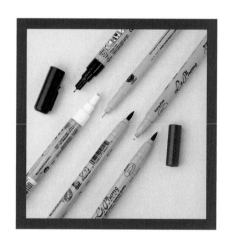

using markers

Markers can be used to color wooden shapes, but most often they are used to accent or add details to a project. Sometimes water-based markers will "bleed" when used over paint and other mediums, therefore permanent markers are recommended when making any of the projects in this book.

Permanent markers are available in a huge assortment of colors. They are available with extra-fine tips to wide tips, and generally are fast drying.

gluing basics

Craft glue is a white, tacky glue that dries clear. The water content in some glues is greater than that in others, so using a good craft glue is important.

When using craft glue on soft-foam sheeting, apply it to the surface of the foam, then allow it to set-up slightly so that it becomes "tacky" to the touch. This will assure that the foam will adhere to itself.

Remember to let the craft glue thoroughly dry before moving on to the next step.

using glitter

Glue is needed when applying glitter, but using as little as possible is always best. In some instances, slightly thinning the glue with water before applying it is recommended.

Apply the watered-down glue to the project with a paintbrush. Hold the project over a sheet of paper and generously sprinkle the area with glitter before the glue has a chance to dry. Shake the project to remove the excess glitter and return the excess glitter to the container.

Allow the glue to thoroughly dry, then repeat if more glitter is desired or if another color is called for.

bending wire

Depending on the type and gauge of wire being used, it is possible to bend and shape the wire with your hands. However, some wire is too hard to bend in this manner and the use of needle-nosed pliers is necessary.

rubber stamping

Using a rubber brayer is considered a rubber stamping tech-nique. When using a brayer to apply ink from an ink pad onto your project, make certain to place a sheet of paper under the project to help protect your work surface from any ink.

Immediately clean the ink from the brayer or it will permanently stain the rubber.

projects requiring supervision

Though these crafts are considered simple, a few of them require the use of tools where supervision is required. Even if a project can be created safely without supervision, make certain you have an adult's per-

mission before beginning your craft project and/or using supplies that are around the house.

Craft knives contain razor type blades that are extremely sharp and must be treated with a great deal of caution. They are used in place of scissors to cut certain items, such as plastic foam, and to get into places that scissors cannot. Remember to always cut away from yourself when using a craft knife.

A drill is used to drill holes in wood and/or plastic. They can be electric or hand-powered, but either type should be used with caution. Secure the item to be drilled, then carefully place the drill bit on the spot where the hole is to be placed. When drilling through thick wood, the drill bit could get hot enough to cause minor burns, so it is important not to touch the drill bit immediately after drilling.

When using an oven or other heat source, care must be taken to avoid serious burns.

cleaning up your work surface

Once your project is finished, you must clean up your work surface and put all of your tools and supplies away.

If your project included painting, sealing, or gluing with a paintbrush, it is very important to thoroughly clean its bristles with water. If you do not, the paintbrush could be ruined and therefore unable to be used on the next project you choose to create.

for best results

Always read and follow the directions on every product label. Even though it might appear that certain products are identical, small differences in them could affect the outcome of your projects.

If you have questions concerning any of the products listed in the materials lists for each project, your local craft store employees are very knowledgable.

As you follow the step-by-step instructions, refer to the colored photographs as often as necessary to aid in the creation of your very own masterpiece!

valentine frame

by **BARB ZIMMERMAN**

Artwork by Landon Sexton

YOU WILL NEED

- Craft glue
- Darning needle
- Decorative-edged scissors: Victorian
- 1/4" Hole punch
- Paintbrush
- Pencil
- Photograph
- (2) Red and white ribbon with hearts, 12" long
- Red mat to fit 8" x 10" frame
- Scissors
- Tape
- Towel
- White card stock

Photo on page 16

1 Trace outline of mat, including center opening, onto card stock.

2 Cut center from card stock.

3 Using decorative-edged scissors, trim outside edges of card stock.

4 Transfer Heart Frame Pattern from page 17 onto card stock.

5 Lay card stock on top of a towel with traced hearts facing upward. Using a darning needle, pierce a line of "dots" through the card stock along traced lines.

6 Using a paintbrush, apply glue to unpierced areas of card stock.

7 Glue card stock to mat. Make certain center openings are perfectly aligned.

8 Punch two holes, 1/2" apart, at top center and bottom center of card stock and mat as shown on pattern. Note: If mat is too wide, it may be necessary to use a drill to make these holes.

9 Thread ribbons through holes in mat, back to front, and tie into bows.

10 Place photo in center opening of mat and hold in place with tape.

"It's love, it's love that makes the world go 'round."

—French song

This project sponsored by: Fiskars®: Hole Punch, Paper Edgers, Scissors

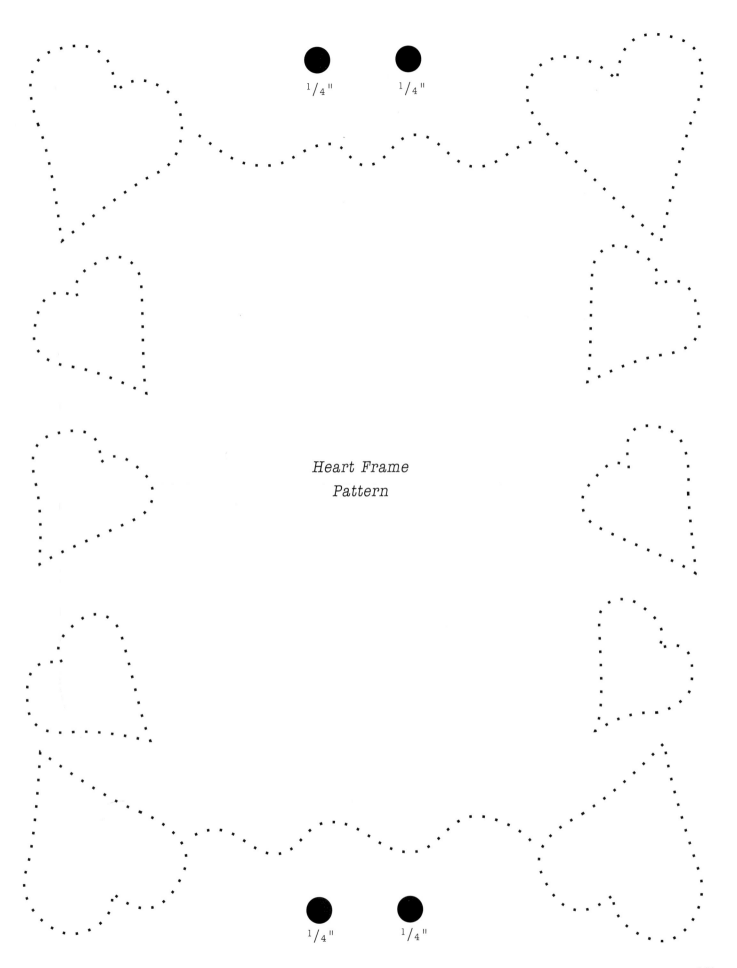

Heart Frame
Pattern

1/4" 1/4"

1/4" 1/4"

17

my love is inside confetti pouch

by CAROL DACE

Artwork by Jaime Schultz

1 Transfer Large Heart Pattern from page 19 onto white card stock.

2 Place plastic sheet on top of white card stock. Cut hearts from card stock and plastic.

3 Keep card stock and plastic hearts together. Using heart punch, punch hearts approximately every $1/4$" around outside edges of card stock and plastic hearts. Save all heart punchouts.

YOU WILL NEED

- Black fine-tip marker
- Blunt-point needle with large eye
- Card stock:
  Red
  White
- Clear plastic sheet
- Heart confetti
- $1/8$" Heart punch
- $1/8$"-wide Red ribbon, 45" long
- Scissors

This project sponsored by: Fiskars®: Heart Punch, Scissors

18

4 Write "My Love Is Inside" in center of white heart with a marker.

5 Transfer Small Heart Pattern at right onto red card stock.

6 Cut out heart.

7 Write your name in center of red heart with the marker.

8 Thread needle with ribbon. Starting at top center, lace card stock and plastic hearts together, leaving a 9" length of ribbon at the beginning and ending. Half way through the lacing process, insert red heart, heart confetti, and heart punchouts that were removed from the edges. Tie ribbon into a bow at top of heart.

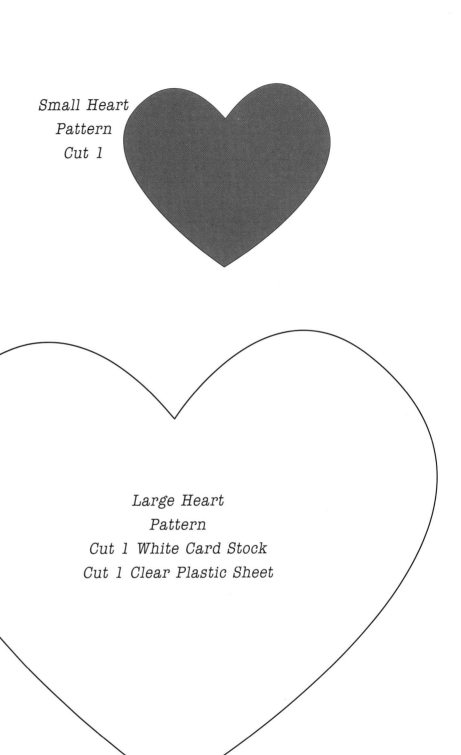

Small Heart Pattern Cut 1

Large Heart Pattern Cut 1 White Card Stock Cut 1 Clear Plastic Sheet

19

hanging bird

by MARY AYRES

Artwork by Jaime Schultz

YOU WILL NEED

- Craft glue
- Decorative-edged scissors:
  Cloud
- Hole punches:
  $1/8$"
  $1/16$"
- Metallic black and silver cord, 33" long
- Opaque pony beads:
  (5) Light blue
  (5) Mint green
  (5) Purple
  (5) White
  (5) Yellow
- Scissors
- Soft-foam sheeting, $1/16$" thick:
  Light blue
  Yellow
- (2) Wiggle eyes, 7mm

1 Transfer Body and Wings Patterns from page 22 onto light blue soft-foam sheeting and Beak Pattern onto yellow.

2 Cut out body, wings, and beak.

3 Using decorative-edged scissors, trim outside edges of wings and tail feathers.

4 Punch holes in body and wings as shown on patterns.

5 To make opening for wings, cut along dashed lines and insert wings.

6 Cut five 5" lengths from cord and make a knot at one end of each length. Place a daub of glue on remaining ends and twist between your fingers to form points. String five beads onto each length of cord in order shown in photo.

7 Thread one beaded cord through each hole along bottom of tail feathers, front to back, and make a knot at each end.

8 Glue eyes and beak in place.

9 To make the hanger, thread remaining length of cord through holes at top of each wing, front to back, and make a knot at each end.

How did the bird pull a muscle? "She forgot to do her worm-ups!"

This project sponsored by: Darice®: Foamies™, Metallic Cord, Pony Beads, Wiggle Eyes; Fiskars®: Hole Punches, Paper Edgers, Scissors

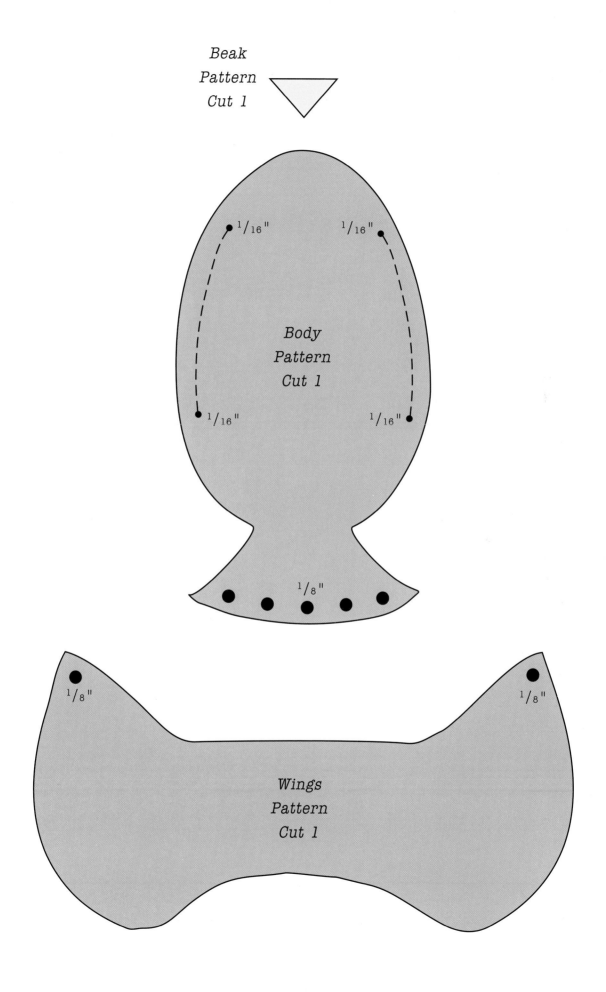

Beak
Pattern
Cut 1

1/16" 1/16"

Body
Pattern
Cut 1

1/16" 1/16"

1/8"

1/8" 1/8"

Wings
Pattern
Cut 1

marbled bead bracelet

by BRENDA SPITZER

Artwork by Jaime Schultz

YOU WILL NEED

- Elastic cord
- Fine-tip opaque markers:
  Turquoise
  White
- Paintbrush
- Scissors
- Tape measure
- Wooden beads:
  (5) $1/2$" dia.
  (10) $3/8$" dia.

1 Measure your wrist, then cut a length of elastic cord the measurement of your wrist plus 1".

2 Color $1/2$"-diameter beads with a white marker and $3/8$"-diameter beads with turquoise.

3 Place beads, one at a time, on the handle of a paintbrush. Draw curvy lines on each white bead with a turquoise marker by holding marker still against bead as you turn paintbrush in random directions. Repeat with turquoise beads and white marker.

4 String beads onto elastic cord and tie ends in a triple knot.

peek-a-boo bunny

by JULIE McGUFFEE

YOU WILL NEED

- Black medium-tip marker
- $1/4$"-wide Blue ribbon, 15" long
- Chenille stems, 10" long:
  (2) Pink, 12mm
  (3) White, 6mm
- Craft glue
- Easter stickers
- $1/4$" Hole punch
- $3/4$" Pink pom-pom
- Plastic-foam egg, 4" high
- Scissors
- Small peat pot, 4" dia. x 3" high
- Small sponge
- White acrylic paint
- White soft-foam sheeting, $1/16$" thick
- (2) Wiggle eyes, 8mm

1 Transfer Ear Pattern from page 25 onto soft-foam sheeting two times.

2 Cut out ears.

3 Cut two 3" lengths from one pink chenille stem. Glue onto each ear as shown in Diagram A below. Dip extended ends into glue and push into top of egg.

4 Cut six 4" pieces from white chenille stems. To make whiskers, push one end of each into front of egg, approximately 1" deep. Bend whiskers back to lie flat against egg.

5 Glue eyes in place.

6 To make the nose, glue pom-pom on top of chenille stems.

7 To make the mouth, draw a vertical line under the nose with a marker.

Diagram A

8 Lightly sponge-paint peat pot with white.

9 Punch holes, spaced approximately $1/2''$ apart, around top edge of pot.

10 Thread ribbon through holes and tie into a bow in the front.

11 Insert ends of remaining pink chenille stem into holes on opposite sides of pot. Bend upward and twist to hold each side in place.

12 Decorate pot with stickers and glue bunny inside pot.

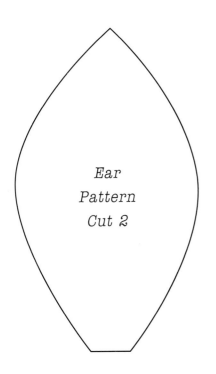

Ear
Pattern
Cut 2

This project sponsored by: Darice®: Chenille Stems, Foamies™, Pom-pom, Wiggle Eyes; Delta Ceramcoat®: Acrylic Paint; Fiskars®: Hole Punch, Scissors; Dow Styrofoam®: Plastic Foam

chicks in a basket

by CAROL DACE

YOU WILL NEED

To make one hen and one rooster:

- Black fine-tip marker
- Chenille stem, $4^1/_2$" long: (1) Red, 6mm
- Cotton swab
- Craft glue
- Feathers:
  Blue
  Red
- Felt:
  Orange
  White
  Yellow
- Pink acrylic paint
- (2) Plastic caps from orange juice containers
- Plastic eggs:
  (1) White
  (1) Yellow
- $^1/_4$"-wide Satin ribbon, any color
- Scissors
- (2) Small buttons

1 To make stands, glue each egg to a plastic cap.

2 Transfer Beak Pattern from right onto orange felt two times, Wing Pattern onto white two times, and onto yellow two times.

3 Cut out beaks and wings.

4 Glue yellow wings to sides of yellow egg and white wings to sides of white egg.

5 Fold beaks in half and glue to eggs.

6 Glue one button on top of each yellow wing and one red feather on top of each white wing.

Beak Pattern Cut 2

Wing Pattern Cut 2 White Cut 2 Yellow

7 Glue several red and blue feathers to back of white egg.

8 Draw eyes on each egg with a marker.

9 To make rosy cheeks, use a cotton swab to apply pink paint to each side of beaks.

10 Tie ribbon into a bow and glue to top of yellow egg (hen) or make a sailor's hat by gluing

26

ribbon in a circle around top of egg.

11 Cut one 3" piece and one 1¹/₂" piece from chenille stem. To make the comb, bend the 3" piece into three bumps as shown in Diagram A below. To make the waddle, bend the 1¹/₂" piece to fit across, down, and back up to beak as shown in Diagram B below.

12 Glue comb to top of white egg (rooster) and waddle to front.

Diagram A

Diagram B

This project sponsored by: Darice®: Chenille Stem, Feathers, Felt; Delta Ceramcoat®: Acrylic Paint; Fiskars®: Scissors

egg ornament

by JULIE McGUFFEE

Artwork by Melissa Worthen

YOU WILL NEED

- Craft glue
- Decorative 2-ply napkin
- Disposable plate
- Gold thread, 6" long
- Iridescent glitter
- 1/4"-wide Light pink ribbon, 12" long
- (2) Mauve ribbon roses
- Mauve tassel, 2" to 4" long
- Paintbrush
- Plastic-foam egg, 3" high
- Quilt pin
- Scissors
- Wooden craft stick

1 Cut out designs from napkin to decorate egg. Carefully pull off the top layer as shown in Diagram A below—this layer has the designs on it.

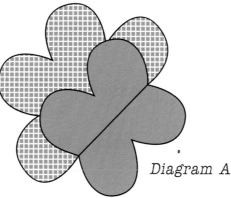

Diagram A

2 To make a handle, push a craft stick into bottom of egg.

3 Pour some glue onto a disposable plate and add a little bit of water to slightly thin the glue. Using a paintbrush, cover entire surface of egg with watered-down glue. While glue is still wet, carefully place napkin cutouts on egg as desired. Gently pat down onto glue.

4 Carefully apply another coat of watered-down glue over entire surface of egg. If napkin tears, push back in place. Tears will not show once glue dries.

5 While glue is still wet, generously sprinkle entire surface of egg with glitter, then shake so excess glitter falls off. Remove craft stick.

6 To make the loop for hanging, place ends of thread together and tie a knot. Tie ribbon into a bow.

7 Push quilt pin through knot in loop, through center of bow, then down into top of egg.

8 Dip ribbon roses into glue and place on top of bow to hide quilt pin.

9 Dip hanging loop at top of tassel into glue and push into hole in bottom of egg where craft stick was placed.

This project sponsored by: Dow Styrofoam®: Plastic Foam; Fiskars®: Scissors

the Lord is my shepherd magnet

by MARY AYRES

YOU WILL NEED

- Adhesive-backed magnetic strip, $2^1/_2$" long
- $^3/_8$" Bell
- Black fine-tip marker
- $^1/_4$"-wide Blue ribbon, 9" long
- Craft glue
- Mini chalkboard with wooden frame, 2" wide x 3" long
- Paintbrush
- Scissors
- White acrylic paint
- White fine-tip opaque marker
- (4) Wooden mini craft sticks
- Wooden shapes:
  (1) Large heart, flat
  (1) Medium heart, flat
  (3) Small teardrops, flat

1 Paint large heart (head), medium heart (face), teardrops (ears and tail), craft sticks (legs), and chalkboard frame (body) with white.

2 Draw swirls around outside edges of head and body, details on face, swirl on tail, and hooves at bottom of legs with a black marker as shown in Diagram A at right.

3 Write "the Lord is my Shepherd" on chalkboard with a white marker. Add a tiny dot to upper inside corners of each eye.

Diagram A

30

4 Glue face to front and ears to back of head, then head to front and tail and legs to back of body.

5 Tie ribbon into a bow. Cut a "V" at ends of ribbon. Glue bow and bell to body below face.

6 Remove backing from magnetic strip and adhere to back of chalk-board.

This project sponsored by: Darice®: Adhesive-backed Magnet Strip, Bell, Chalkboard; Delta Ceramcoat®: Acrylic Paint; Fiskars®: Scissors; Forster®: Craft Stick Minis, Woodsies™; Sakura of America: Identipen™, Permapaque™ Opaque Pigment Marker

flying bee frame

by MARY AYRES

Artwork by Sammy Hadnagy

YOU WILL NEED

- Acrylic paints:
  Blue
  Yellow
- Black fine-tip marker
- $9/16$"-dia. Circle punch
- (6) $5/8$"-dia. Clear flat-backed glass beads
- Craft glue
- Paintbrush
- Paper frame, 6" wide x $7^1/_2$" high
- White card stock
- (6) Wiggle eyes, 5mm
- (3) Wooden mini craft sticks

This project sponsored by: Darice®: Glass Beads, Wiggle Eyes; Delta Ceramcoat®: Acrylic Paints; Fiskars®: Circle Punch

1 Paint frame with blue and craft sticks (bees) with yellow.

2 Draw flight path on frame with a marker as shown on Bee Flight Pattern below.

3 Draw an outline around outside edges of and zigzag stripes on each bee as shown in Diagram A below.

4 Punch six circles (wings) from card stock. Draw details on all wings as shown in Diagram B below.

5 Glue eyes in place.

6 Glue bees and wings to frame. Glue glass beads on top of wings.

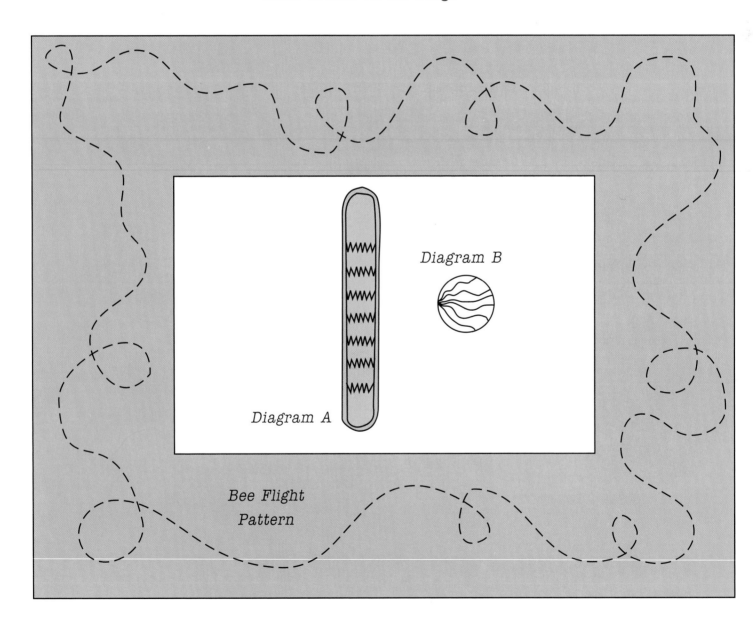

Diagram A

Diagram B

Bee Flight Pattern

bunny mask

by BARB ZIMMERMAN

Artwork by Nick Pepe

YOU WILL NEED

- Black fine-tip marker
- Craft glue
- Elastic cord
- $1/8$" Hole punch
- $3/4$" Pink pom-pom
- Scissors
- Soft-foam sheeting, $1/16$" thick:
  Gray
  Pink
  White

1 Transfer Face Pattern from page 36 onto gray soft-foam sheeting one time, Ear 1 Pattern onto gray two times, Ear 2 Pattern onto pink two times, Ear 3 and Cheek Patterns onto white two times, and Teeth Pattern onto white one time.

2 Cut out face, ears, cheeks, and teeth. Carefully cut out holes in face.

3 Punch one hole at each side of face as shown on pattern.

4 Layer and glue white, pink, and gray sections of ears together, then glue layered ears to back of face as shown in Diagram A below.

5 Glue cheeks to front and teeth to back of face.

6 To make the nose, glue pom-pom at center of face where cheeks meet.

7 Draw eyelashes on face, whiskers on cheeks, and vertical line on teeth with a marker.

8 Thread elastic cord through holes, back to front, on each side of mask. Adjust elastic cord to desired length and make a knot at each end.

Diagram A

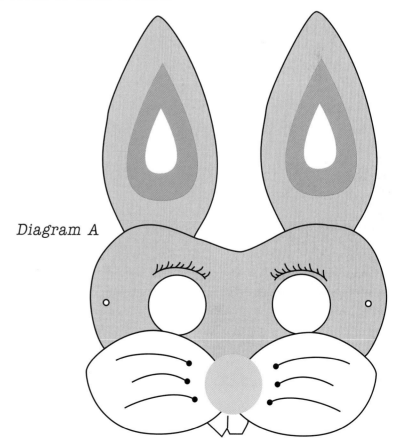

34

This project sponsored by: Darice®: Foamies™, Pom-pom; Fiskars®: Hole Punch, Scissors

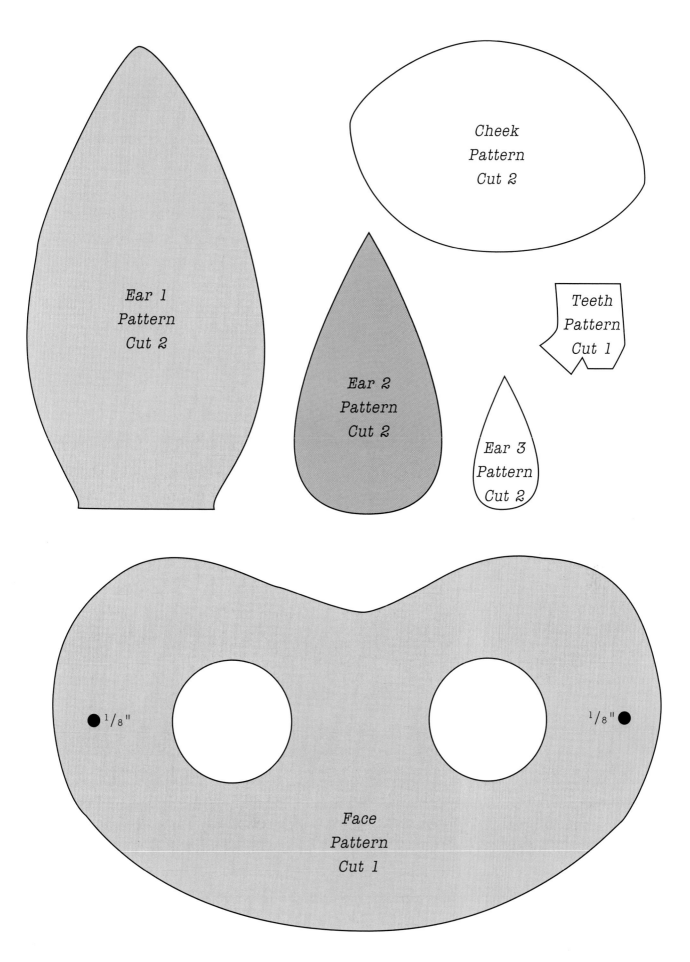

Ear 1
Pattern
Cut 2

Cheek
Pattern
Cut 2

Ear 2
Pattern
Cut 2

Teeth
Pattern
Cut 1

Ear 3
Pattern
Cut 2

Face
Pattern
Cut 1

● $1/8''$ $1/8''$ ●

pom-pom caterpillar

by **JULIE McGUFFEE**

Artwork by Rebecca Hendricks

YOU WILL NEED

- Chenille stem, 10" long: (1) Green, 12mm
- Craft glue
- 3/4" Green pom-poms, (approx. 16)
- Green soft-foam sheeting, 1/16" thick
- Scissors
- (2) Wiggle eyes, 7mm

1 Cut a 1/2"-wide by 10"-long strip from soft-foam sheeting.

2 Glue chenille stem to one side of soft-foam strip.

3 Glue pom-poms to opposite side of soft-foam strip.

4 Glue eyes in place.

5 To form the caterpillar, bend chenille stem. As caterpillar is bent, gaps may appear between pom-poms. Additional pom-poms can be glued into these gaps.

This project sponsored by: Darice®: Chenille Stem, Foamies™, Pom-poms, Wiggle Eyes; Fiskars®: Scissors

fly-away magnets

by CHERYL BALL

Artwork by Kaela Eddy

YOU WILL NEED

To make one butterfly, one dragonfly, and one bumblebee:

- Acrylic paints:
  Black
  Blue
  Bright pink
  Dark lavender
  Light blue
  Light green
  Light pink
  Orange
  White
  Yellow
- Adhesive-backed magnetic strip, 3" long
- Black fine-tip marker
- (3) 24-gauge Black wire, 4" long
- Craft glue
- Craft snips
- Needle-nosed pliers
- Paintbrush
- Scissors
- White fine-tip opaque marker
- (6) Wiggle eyes, 4mm
- (9) Wooden craft spoons

1 Paint one craft spoon with bright pink, one with blue, one black with yellow stripes, and two with white.

2 Paint top halves of two craft spoons with orange and bottom halves with yellow.

3 Paint top halves of two craft spoons with light green and bottom halves with dark lavender.

4 Using the end of the paintbrush handle, paint dots for cheeks on the bright pink (butterfly), blue (dragonfly), and black and yellow striped (bumblebee) craft spoons with light pink. Paint dots on butterfly's body with dark lavender.

5 Draw a nose and a mouth on butterfly and dragonfly with a black marker.

6 Draw a nose and a mouth on bumblebee with a white marker.

7 Paint a large dot at top of each orange/yellow craft spoons (butterfly wings) with light green. Paint a wavy line from dot to center of wings with light green. Paint a large dot at bottom of each wing with bright pink. Paint a wavy line from dot to center of wings with bright pink.

8 Paint horizontal wavy lines down dragonfly's body with light green. Paint horizontal lines in between the wavy lines with bright pink.

9 Using the end of the paintbrush handle, paint dots at top of each light

green/dark lavender craft spoons (dragonfly wings) with yellow. Paint dots at bottom of each wing with bright pink. Paint dots at top of each white craft spoon (bumblebee wings) with light blue.

10 Randomly draw dots inside yellow stripes on bumblebee's body with the black marker.

11 Using craft snips, cut approximately 1" from bottoms of bumblebee wings. Discard cut-off pieces.

12 Glue eyes in place.

13 Glue matching wings together, then glue appropriate bodies to tops of wings.

14 To make the antennae, bend each length of wire in half and curl each end with needle-nosed pliers, then glue in place.

15 Cut magnetic strip into three 1" lengths.

16 Remove backing from magnetic strips and adhere to backs of butterfly, dragonfly, and bumblebee.

This project sponsored by: Darice®: Adhesive-backed Magnet Strip, Wiggle Eyes, Wire; Delta Ceramcoat®: Acrylic Paints; Fiskars®: Scissors, Softouch Craft Snips; Forster®: Craft Spoons

cow bookmark by DIMPLES MUCHERINO

Artwork by Jack Deaton

YOU WILL NEED

- Acrylic paints:
  Black
  Gray
  Pink
  White
- ⁵/₈" Bell
- Black fine-point marker
- Craft glue
- Natural raffia strand, 12" long
- Paintbrush
- Wooden jumbo craft stick
- Wooden shapes:
  (1) Large egg, flat
  (1) Medium oval, flat
  (2) Small ovals, flat
  (2) Small teardrops, flat

1 Paint craft stick (body) and egg (head) with white, medium oval (muzzle) with pink, small ovals (ears) with black, and teardrops (horns) with gray.

2 Randomly paint spots on body with black.

3 Draw eyes, nostrils, mouth, line on craft stick to make legs, hair on top of head, and dashed lines around horns, head, and muzzle with a marker.

4 Glue head to top front of body, muzzle to head, and ears and horns to back of head.

5 String bell onto raffia. Wrap raffia around craft stick below muzzle, tie into a bow, and glue to craft stick.

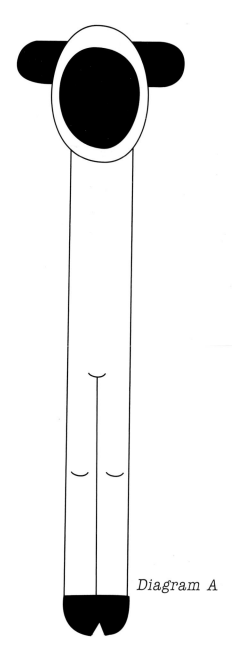

Diagram A

Other farm animals can also be created. Use Diagram A above to make a sheep.

This project sponsored by: Darice®: Bell, Raffia; Delta Ceramcoat®: Acrylic Paints; Forster®: Craft Stick, Woodsies™

rainbow suncatcher

by JULIE McGUFFEE

Artwork by Katie Reed

YOU WILL NEED

- Chenille stems, 10" long: (6) White, 6mm
- Cookie sheet
- Faceted plastic beads:
  (17) Blue
  (13) Green
  (6) Orange
  (21) Purple
  (26) Red
  (9) Yellow
- Monofilament, 12" long
- Scissors
- Waxed paper

1 String orange beads onto a chenille stem, making certain all beads are touching. Bend the chenille stem into a "U" shape.

2 Continue stringing each color of beads onto separate chenille stems. Bend each stem into a "U" shape.

3 Trim chenille stems so they are even with the beads at each end.

4 Line a cookie sheet with waxed paper. Starting with the orange beads, place rows of beads on cookie sheet as shown in Diagram A below, making certain all rows of beads are as close together as possible.

5 Place cookie sheet into a cold oven. Turn oven to bake at 350º. When oven has reached 350º, "bake" for 10 minutes to fuse beads together, then turn oven off. Let oven cool completely, then remove cookie sheet.

6 Carefully remove beaded rainbow from waxed paper.

7 To make the loop for hanging, carefully thread monofilament at top center through the space between rows of red and purple beads and tie ends in a knot.

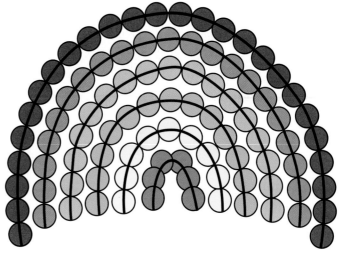

Diagram A

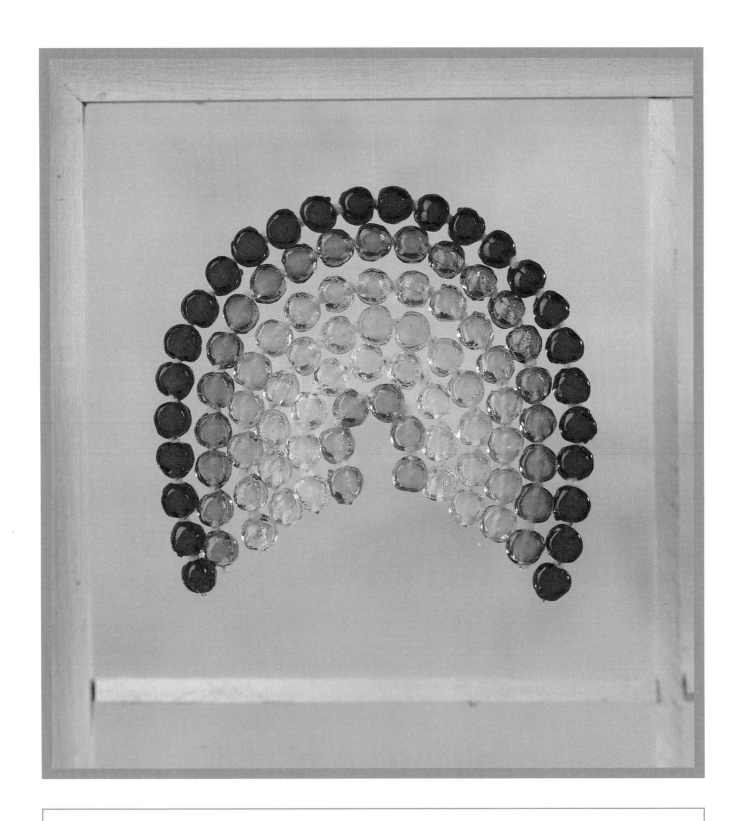

This project sponsored by: Darice®: Chenille Stems, Faceted
Plastic Beads, Monofilament; Fiskars®: Scissors

flowerpot wind chime

by **JULIE McGUFFEE**

Artwork by Melissa Worthen

YOU WILL NEED

- Acrylic paints:
  Black
  Light blue
  Moss green
  Pink
  Red
  White
- Black extrafine-tip marker
- Black soft-foam sheeting, $^1/_{16}$" thick
- Cotton swab
- Craft glue
- Paintbrush
- Pink powder blush
- Scissors
- Small clay pot, $3^1/_2$" dia. x $3^1/_2$" high
- Small wind chime assembly with oval clapper
- White extrafine-tip opaque marker
- Wooden shapes:
  (2) Medium hearts, flat
  (2) Small circles, flat
  (1) Small heart, flat
  (3) Small teardrops, flat

1 Paint clay pot and circles (cat's pupils) with black, wind chime clapper (bird's body) and medium hearts (bird's wings) with light blue, two teardrops (cat's eyes) with white, bottoms of eyes with moss green, one teardrop (cat's tongue) with pink, and small heart (cat's nose) with red.

2 Transfer Ear Pattern from below onto soft-foam sheeting two times.

3 Cut out ears. Cut along dashed line on each ear as shown on pattern.

4 Glue ears to pot. The cut in the center of each ear will allow it to be glued to top and sides of pot.

5 Glue bird's wings to back of bird's body as shown in Diagram A on page 46.

Ear Pattern
Cut 2

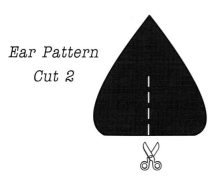

What do you feed your cat for breakfast? "Mice Krispies and Shredded Tweet!"

This project sponsored by: Darice®: Foamies™; Delta Ceramcoat®: Acrylic Paints; Fiskars®: Scissors; Forster®: Woodsies™

6 Draw two small dots for bird's eyes and a small diamond for bird's beak with a black marker.

7 To make breast feathers, use a cotton swab to rub blush on bird's body. Color in bird's beak with blush.

8 Glue cat's pupils to cat's eyes and cat's eyes, nose, and tongue to pot as shown in Diagram B at right.

9 Draw eyebrows, whiskers, and mouth on pot with a white marker. Add a tiny dot to each pupil.

10 Place a generous amount of glue on top of wooden disk at top of wind chime. Pull loop at top of wind chime assembly through hole in bottom of pot. Make certain the disk fits snugly against bottom of pot.

11 Use loop at top of wind chime assembly to hang wind chime.

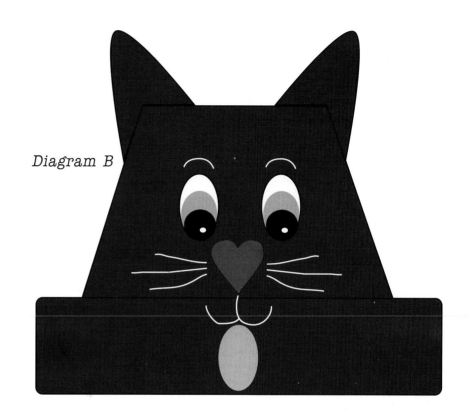

Diagram B

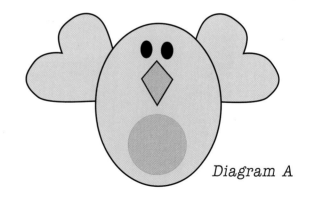

Diagram A

garden necklace by BARB ZIMMERMAN

Artwork by Kaela Eddy

YOU WILL NEED

- Acrylic paints:
  White
  Yellow
- Fine-tip markers:
  Assorted colors
- Paintbrush

- (6) White opaque heart pony beads
- (5) $^3/_4$"-dia. Wooden spools
- $^1/_8$"-wide Yellow satin ribbon, 24" long

1 Paint two spools with yellow and three spools with white.

2 Using colored markers, decorate each spool with flowers and leaves as desired.

3 String beads and spools onto ribbon in order shown in photo. Adjust ribbon to desired length and tie ends together in a knot.

This project sponsored by: Darice®: Pony Beads, Wooden Spools; Delta Ceramcoat®: Acrylic Paints

world's greatest dad plaque

by **MARY AYRES**

Artwork by Heidi Hansen

YOU WILL NEED

- Acrylic paints:
  Brown
  Light brown
- Black fine-tip marker
- Craft glue
- Drill with $1/8$" bit
- Natural jute, 12" long
- Paintbrush
- White fine-tip opaque marker
- (10) Wooden mini craft sticks
- Wooden plaque, $2^3/4$" wide x $7^1/4$" long

1 Drill holes in top corners of plaque.

2 Paint plaque with brown and craft sticks with light brown.

3 Draw wood grain lines on each craft stick with a black marker. Make certain to make each one a little different as no two pieces of wood are identical.

4 Glue craft sticks on plaque spelling the word "DAD."

5 Write "world's greatest" inside the top of the letter "A" with a white marker.

6 To make the hanger, thread jute through holes at top of plaque, front to back, and make a knot at each end.

Personalize a plaque with your name on it for your bedroom door or school locker.

This project sponsored by: Delta Ceramcoat®: Acrylic Paints; Fiskars®: Hand Drill, Scissors; Forster®: Craft Stick Minis, Wooden Slat

giraffe switchplate cover

by **MARY AYRES**

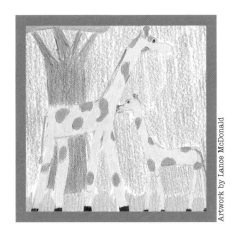

YOU WILL NEED

- Acrylic paints:
  Orange
  Yellow
- Fine-tip markers:
  Black
  Brown
- Chenille stem,
  $6^1/_4$" long:
  (1) Orange, 6mm
- Craft glue
- $1/_{16}$" Hole punch
- Paintbrush
- Paper switchplate
  cover, $2^3/_4$" wide x
  $4^1/_2$" high
- Scissors
- Wooden craft spoon
- (4) Wooden craft
  sticks
- Wooden shapes:
  (1) 2" Oval, flat
  (2) Small teardrops,
  flat

1 Paint switchplate cover (body), teardrops (ears), oval (head), craft spoon (neck), and craft sticks (legs) with orange.

2 Draw eyes and nostrils on head and hooves at bottom of legs with a black marker as shown in Diagram A below.

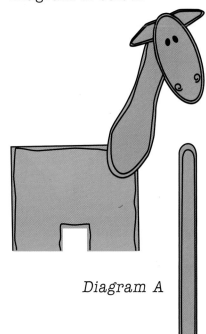

Diagram A

3 Draw an outline around outside edges of ears, head, neck, body, and legs and around opening on body with a brown marker.

4 Glue ears to back of head, then to front of narrowest end of neck. Glue widest end of neck and legs to front of body.

5 Punch one hole in top left-hand corner of body.

6 To make the tail, cut one 5" length from chenille stem. Make a knot at one end. Thread other end through hole in body, front to back, and bend upward to hold in place.

7 To make horns, bend remaining piece of chenille stem in half. Glue horns to back of head in between ears.

8 Using the end of the paintbrush handle, paint dots on giraffe with yellow. Paint small dots on head and legs and large dots on neck and body.

This project sponsored by: Darice®: Chenille Stem; Delta Ceramcoat®: Acrylic Paints;
Fiskars®: Hole Punch, Scissors; Forster®: Craft Spoon, Craft Sticks, Woodsies™

fish mask

by BARB ZIMMERMAN

Artwork by Melissa Worthen

YOU WILL NEED

- Black fine-tip marker
- Card stock:
  Blue
  Green
  Orange
  Red
  White
  Yellow
- Craft glue
- Elastic cord
- ¹/₈" Hole punch
- Scissors

1 Transfer Face Pattern from page 54 onto green card stock one time, Front Fin and Mouth 2 Patterns onto orange one time, Side Fin Pattern onto blue two times, Mouth 1 Pattern onto yellow one time, Scales 1 Pattern onto yellow two times, Scales 2 Pattern onto red two times, and Scales 3 Pattern onto white two times.

2 Cut out face, front fin, side fins, mouths, and scales. Carefully cut out holes in face.

3 Layer and glue orange and yellow sections of mouth together, then glue layered mouth and front fin to front of face as shown in Diagram A below.

4 Layer and glue side fins and yellow, red, and white scales together, then glue layered fins and scales to front of face.

5 Punch one hole at each side of face as shown on pattern.

6 Draw eyelashes and scales on face and details on yellow, red, and white scales with a marker.

7 Thread elastic cord through holes, back to front, on each side of mask. Adjust elastic cord to desired length and make a knot at each end.

Diagram A

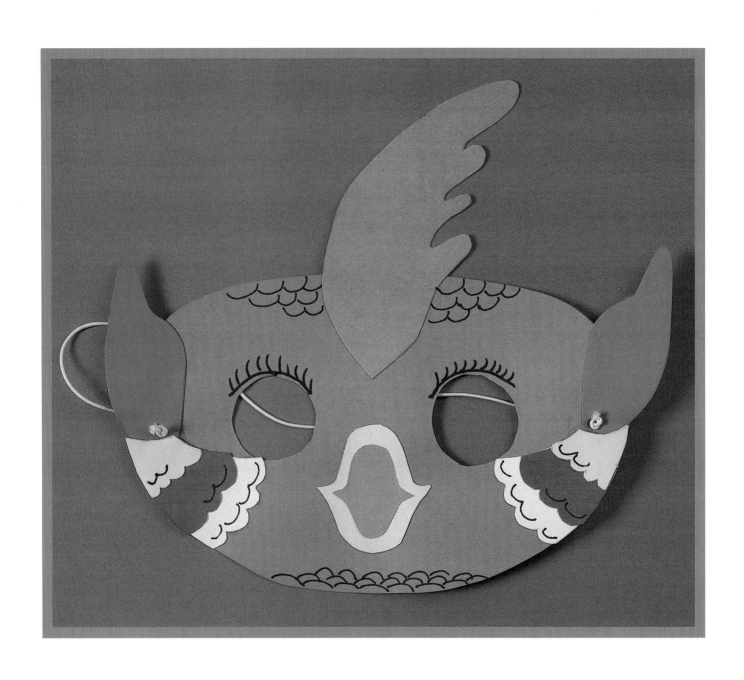

Why is it so easy to weigh fish?
"Because they have their own scales!"

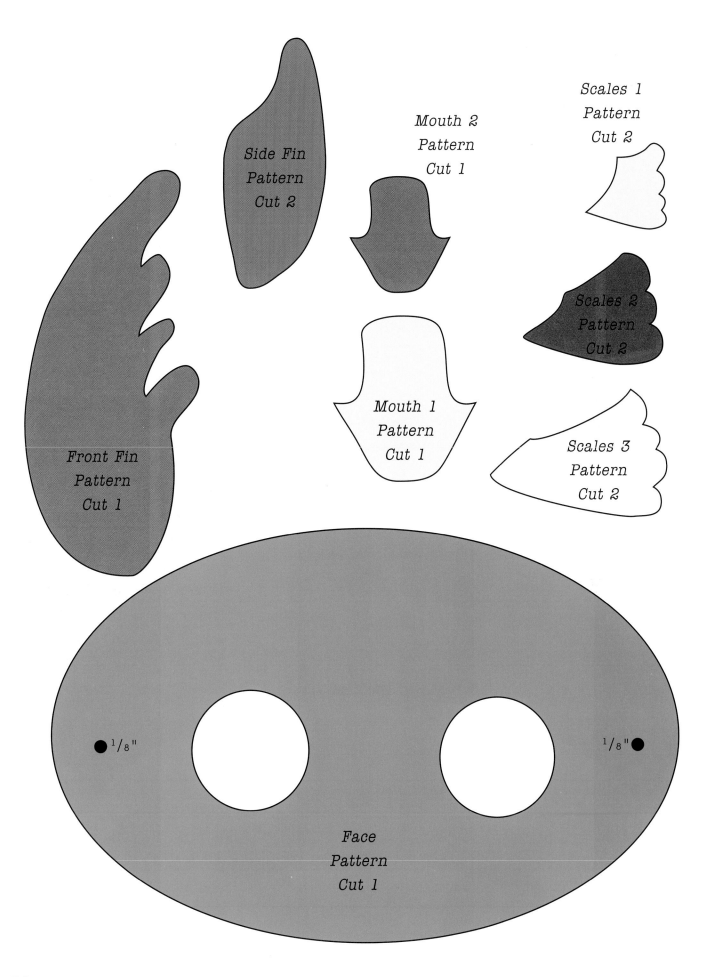

Side Fin
Pattern
Cut 2

Mouth 2
Pattern
Cut 1

Scales 1
Pattern
Cut 2

Scales 2
Pattern
Cut 2

Front Fin
Pattern
Cut 1

Mouth 1
Pattern
Cut 1

Scales 3
Pattern
Cut 2

●1/8"

1/8"●

Face
Pattern
Cut 1

water bottle cover

by JULIE McGUFFEE

YOU WILL NEED

- Black fine-tip marker
- Craft glue
- Decorative-edged scissors: Long Cloud
- Empty water bottle
- $1/8$" Hole punch
- Paper
- Precut soft-foam shapes:
  (1) Dolphin
  (4) Fish
- Ruler
- Scissors
- Soft-foam sheeting, $1/16$" thick:
  Dark blue
  Light blue
- Tape
- White plastic lacing

1 To measure light blue soft-foam sheeting, wrap it around water bottle. Mark appropriate height and length on soft-foam with a marker. Lay soft-foam flat and make a rectangle, using the marks as your guide, adding $3/4$" to length so soft-foam can overlap at the seam as shown in Diagram A below.

Diagram A

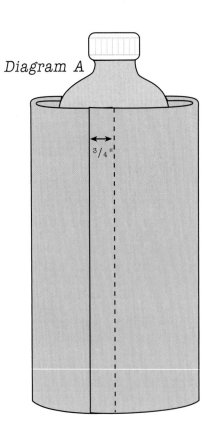

$3/4$"

2 Cut out rectangle.

3 Place water bottle in an upright position on the remaining light blue soft-foam sheeting. Trace around base of water bottle with the marker.

4 Cut out circle.

5 Using the length of rectangle as a pattern, cut two 1"-wide strips from dark blue soft-foam sheeting and one 1"-wide strip from paper. You will not need the additional $3/4$" length since strips will not be overlapped. Set paper strip aside.

6 Using decorative-edged scissors, trim along one long side of each soft-foam strip.

Photo on page 56

This project sponsored by: Darice®: Foamies™; Fiskars®: Hole Punch, Paper Edgers, Scissors; Toner Plastics™: Craft Lace™

7 Align and glue straight edge of one soft-foam strip with straight edge along top of rectangle. Align and glue straight edge of remaining soft-foam strip with straight edge along bottom of rectangle.

8 Fold paper strip in half and make a mark at crease (this should be at center). Fold strip in half three more times to divide into 16 sections. Make a mark at each crease.

9 Lay paper pattern along straight edge of strips. Make 16 dots on each strip, positioned $1/2$" from top edge.

10 Punch one hole at each dot.

11 Using the light blue soft-foam circle as a pattern, cut one circle from paper. Use the same folding technique as described in Step 8 to divide the circle into 16 sections.

12 Lay paper pattern on top of circle. Make 16 dots on circle, positioned $1/2$" from outside edge.

13 Punch one hole at each dot.

14 Starting at one end, lace soft-foam rectangle to soft-foam circle by holding one end of plastic lacing at back of circle as shown in Diagram B below. Thread remaining end up through first hole in circle, then push it out through first hole in rectangle from back. Thread it up through second hole in circle, then push it out through second hole in rectangle. Continue until circle is attached. Tie ends in a knot. As you lace the rectangle and circle together, place circle inside edges of rectangle.

15 Spread glue along inside of overlapping edge of cover and place water bottle inside. Overlap edges and hold in place with tape. Let glue dry, then remove tape.

16 Remove water bottle, then lace along top edge of cover as shown in Diagram C below.

17 Glue precut soft-foam shapes around center of cover.

Diagram B

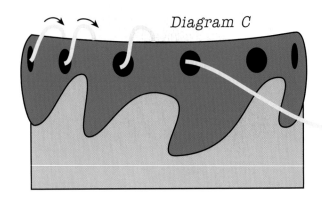

Diagram C

handy sunglasses and penny pocket

by JULIE McGUFFEE

Artwork by Nick Pepe

YOU WILL NEED

To make sunglasses:

- Craft glue
- Flower punches:
  Large
  Medium
- $1/4$" Hole punch
- Plastic sunglasses
- Scissors
- Soft-foam sheeting, $1/16$" thick:
  Orange
  Red
  White
- (2) Wiggle eyes, 15mm

These projects sponsored by: Darice®: Foamies™, Pony Bead, Wiggle Eyes; Fiskars®: Hole Punch, Scissors; Toner Plastics™: Craft Lace™

To make sunglasses:

1 Transfer Hand Pattern from below onto orange soft-foam sheeting two times.

2 Cut out hands.

3 Punch two large flowers from white soft-foam sheeting and two medium flowers from red.

4 Punch ten circles from white soft-foam sheeting.

5 Glue one circle to end of each finger and thumb. Make certain hands are going in opposite directions.

6 Glue large flowers to hands and medium flowers to large flowers.

7 Glue eyes in place.

8 Glue hands to corners of sunglasses.

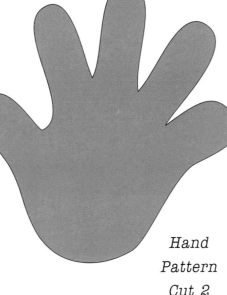

Hand Pattern Cut 2

To make penny pocket:

1 Punch one large flower and one medium flower from soft-foam sheeting.

2 Using scissors, pierce a small hole in lid of film container and in center of each flower.

3 Glue medium flower to large flower.

4 Fold plastic lacing in half and tie ends together in an overhand knot. Push folded end through hole in lid, then through flowers and bead. Tightly pull plastic lacing upward so knot is against bottom of lid and flowers are on top as shown in Diagram A below.

5 Decorate film container with stickers.

Diagram A

brayered bookmarks by MARY AYRES

Artwork by Heidi Hansen

1 Load streamer brayer from rainbow ink pad and roll over one white card stock rectangle. Load mesh brayer from rainbow ink pad and roll over remaining white rectangle.

2 Cut rectangles into $1^1/_2$"-wide by $5^1/_2$"-long rectangles and set aside.

3 Using decorative-edged scissors, trim one long edge of blue and purple $2^1/_4$"-wide by 6"-long rectangles. Trim around outside edges of blue and purple $3^1/_2$"-wide x 7"-long rectangles.

4 Punch ovals along decorative-edged sides of smaller blue and purple rectangles.

YOU WILL NEED

To make two bookmarks:

- Card stock:
  - (1) Blue,
    $2^1/_4$" wide x
    6" long
  - (1) Blue,
    $3^1/_2$" wide x
    7" long
  - (1) Purple,
    $2^1/_4$" wide x
    6" long
  - (1) Purple,
    $3^1/_2$" wide x
    7" long
  - (2) White,
    3" wide x
    7" long
- Decorative-edged scissors:
  Wave

- Glue stick
- $^1/_4$" Hole punch
- $^5/_{16}$" Oval punch
- Pony beads, translucent:
  - (4) Blue
  - (4) Green
  - (4) Pink
  - (4) Purple
- Rainbow ink pad
- Rubber brayers with handles:
  Mesh
  Streamer
- Ruler
- Scissors
- (2) White cords, 12" long

5 Glue mesh-brayered rectangle to smaller decorative-edged purple rectangle, then to larger blue rectangle. Glue streamer-brayered rectangle to smaller blue rectangle, then to larger purple rectangle.

6 Punch one hole at the top center of each bookmark.

7 Thread both ends of each cord through holes, back to front, and pull ends through loop formed by cord.

8 Tie a knot in each cord 1" from tops of bookmarks. Separate cords and string beads onto ends in order shown in photo. Tie a knot in each cord against last beads.

This project sponsored by: Darice®: Pony Beads; Fiskars®: Brayer Rollers and Handle, Glue Stick, Hole Punch, Oval Punch, Paper Edgers, Pigment Stamp Pad, Scissors

turtle mousepad by BARB ZIMMERMAN

Artwork by Landon Sexton

YOU WILL NEED

- Black fine-tip marker
- Black medium-tip marker
- Craft glue
- Dark green card stock
- Green soft-foam sheeting, $1/16$" thick
- Scissors
- (2) Wiggle eyes, 12mm

1 Transfer Body Pattern from page 64 onto soft-foam sheeting two times, Head and Tail Patterns onto card stock one time, and Foot Pattern onto card stock four times.

2 Cut out body, head, feet, and tail.

3 Draw a mouth on head with a fine-tip marker as shown on pattern.

4 Draw design on one soft-foam body with a medium-tip marker as shown on pattern.

5 Glue head, feet, and tail to top of remaining soft-foam body, then glue bodies together.

6 Glue eyes in place.

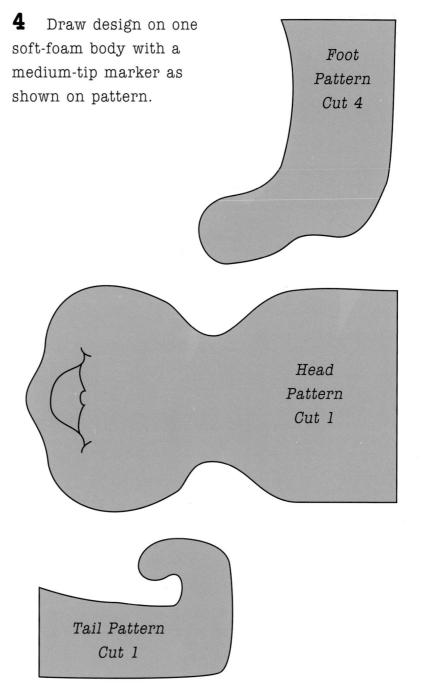

Foot Pattern Cut 4

Head Pattern Cut 1

Tail Pattern Cut 1

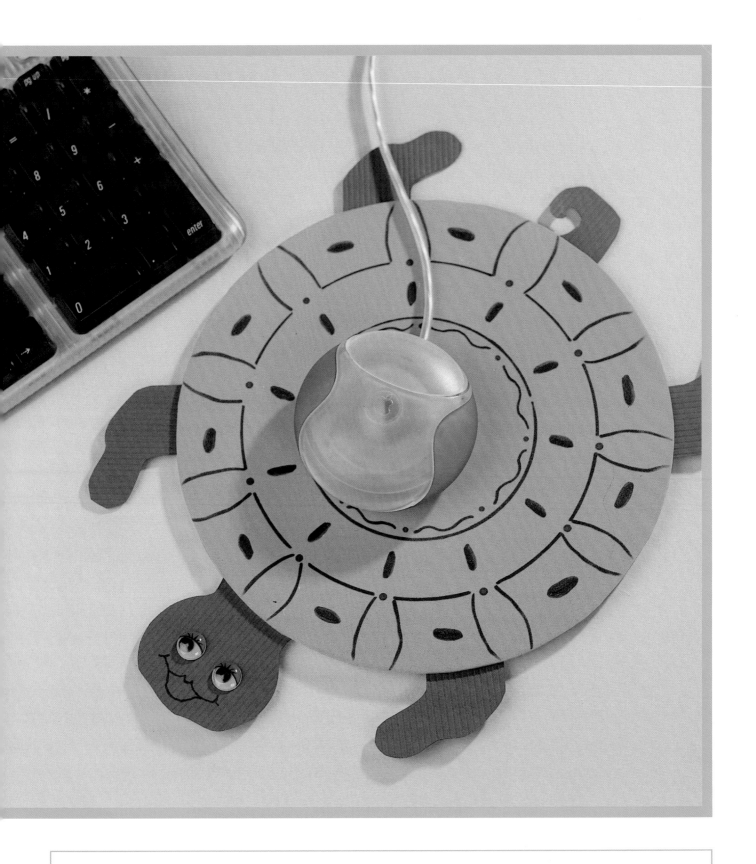

This project sponsored by: Darice®: Foamies™, Wiggle Eyes; Fiskars®: Scissors

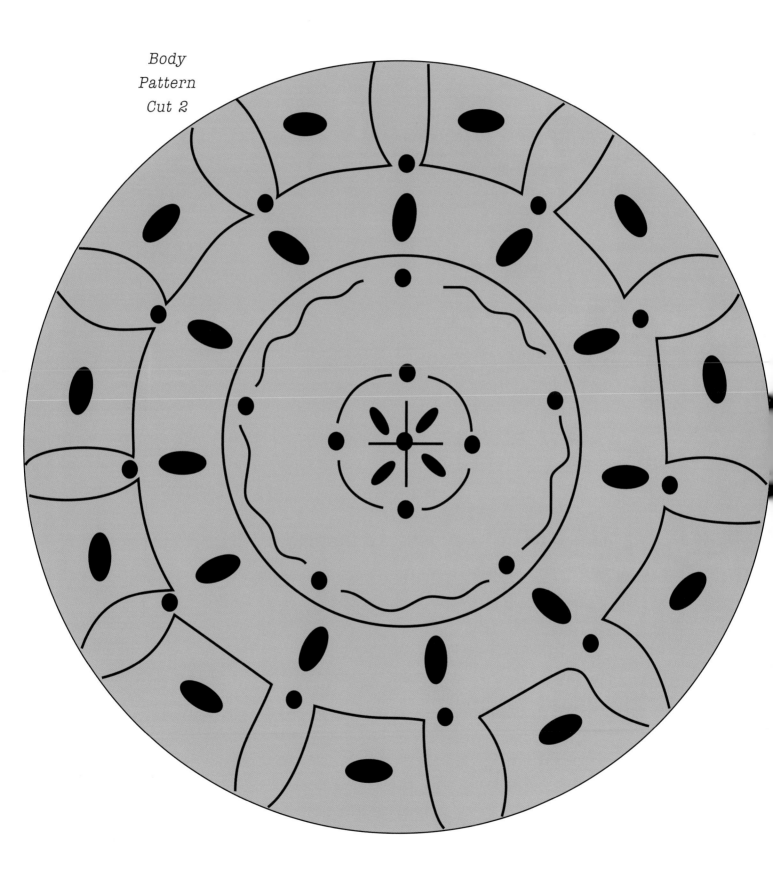

Body
Pattern
Cut 2

64

bear birthday party

by MARY AYRES

Artwork by Melissa Worthen

Photo on page 66

To make treat sack:

1 Transfer Ear Pattern from page 67 onto brown wavy-ridged paper two times, Muzzle Pattern onto yellow straight-ridged paper one time, and Nose Pattern onto black card stock one time.

2 Cut out ears, muzzle, and nose.

3 Using decorative-edged scissors, trim muzzle.

4 Using circle punch, punch one circle from white card stock.

5 Fold top of sack over $1^1/_4$" toward back.

YOU WILL NEED

To make one treat sack, one cupcake topper, and one straw cover:

- Brown lunch sack
- Brown wavy-ridged paper
- Card stock:
  Black
  White
- $^9/_{16}$"-dia. Circle punch
- Craft glue
- Decorative-edged scissors:
  Mini pinking
- $^1/_4$" Hole punch
- Orange cords:
  (2) 7" long
  (1) 15" long
- Scissors
- Treats
- Wiggle eyes:
  (4) 7mm
  (2) 15mm
- Wooden craft pick
- Yellow straight-ridged paper
- Yellow straw

---

6 Using hole punch, punch two holes, 1" apart, at top center of sack.

7 Glue ears and muzzle to front of sack, nose to muzzle, and white circle to nose.

8 Glue eyes in place.

9 Fill sack with treats, fold top of sack over, thread 15" length of cord through holes in sack, back to front, and tie into a bow.

To make cupcake topper:

1 Transfer Bear Pattern (without tabs) from page 67 onto brown wavy-ridged paper one time and Nose Pattern (to be used for muzzle) onto yellow straight-ridged paper one time.

2 Cut out bear and muzzle.

3 Using decorative-edged scissors, trim muzzle.

This project sponsored by: Bemiss-Jason: Construction Paper, Corobuff®, Wavy Ridges™ Paper; Darice®: Cord, Wiggle Eyes; Fiskars®: Circle Punch, Hole Punch, Paper Edgers, Scissors

4 Using circle punch, punch one circle (to be used for nose) from black card stock.

5 Using hole punch, punch one circle from white card stock.

6 Glue muzzle to bear, nose to muzzle, and the white circle to nose.

7 Glue eyes in place.

8 Tie one 7" length of cord into a bow and glue to bottom of bear.

9 Glue rounded end of craft pick vertically to back of bear, leaving 2" of pick extending from bottom.

To make straw cover:

1 Follow directions as described in Steps 1–8 on pages 65 and at left for making cupcake topper, leaving Bear Pattern tabs in place.

2 Using hole punch, punch one hole in center of top and bottom tabs on bear.

3 Bend tabs toward back and insert straw through holes in tabs so straw is at back of bear.

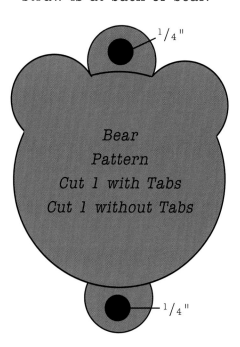

1/4"

Bear Pattern Cut 1 with Tabs Cut 1 without Tabs

1/4"

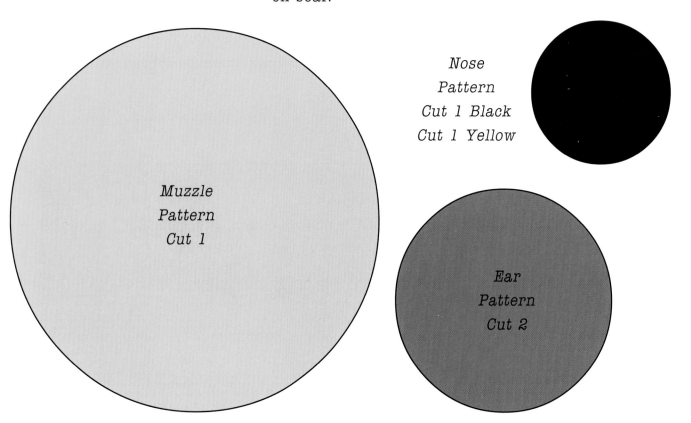

Muzzle Pattern Cut 1

Nose Pattern Cut 1 Black Cut 1 Yellow

Ear Pattern Cut 2

jointed tiger

by MARY AYRES

YOU WILL NEED

- Black medium-tip marker
- $1/8$" Hole punch
- Orange soft-foam sheeting, $1/16$" thick
- (3) Round-headed fasteners
- Scissors

1 Transfer Body and Tail Patterns from below and at right one time and Leg Pattern four times onto orange soft-foam sheeting.

2 Draw an outline around outside edges of body, tail, and legs with a marker. Draw face on head and stripes on head, body, tail, and legs. Make certain to make each one a little different as no two stripes are identical.

3 Cut out body, tail, and legs.

4 Punch three holes in body and one hole at tops of tail and each leg as shown on patterns.

5 Assemble tiger by inserting one fastener into hole at top of one leg, then through appropriate hole in body, then through one more leg. Repeat for remaining legs. To attach tail, insert one fastener into appropriate hole in body, then through hole in tail. Bend fastener prongs flat in back.

Tail Pattern
Cut 1

Body
Pattern
Cut 1

Leg
Pattern
Cut 4

This project sponsored by: Darice®: Foamies™; Fiskars®: Hole Punch, Scissors

fanciful fans

by **BARB ZIMMERMAN**

Artwork by Lance McDonald

YOU WILL NEED

To make one fan:

- Craft glue
- Decorative-edged scissors: Victorian
- Fine-tip opaque markers: Assorted colors
- Paintbrush
- $1/8$"-wide Satin ribbon, 12" long
- Scissors
- Stickers
- Tissue paper, any color and pattern
- White poster board
- (2) Wooden jumbo craft sticks

1 Transfer Fan Pattern from page 72 onto poster board.

2 Cut out fan.

3 Using a paintbrush, apply glue around outside edges of one side of fan. Glue tissue paper to this side of fan. Repeat on opposite side.

4 Using decorative-edged scissors, trim outside edges of fan.

5 Color both sides of craft sticks with colored markers.

6 Decorate one side of each craft stick with markers or stickers as desired.

7 Wrap ribbon around top of one craft stick, tie into a bow, and glue to craft stick. If desired, several colors of ribbon can be combined and tied as one into a bow.

8 To make the handle, apply glue to backs of each craft stick. Place top half of craft stick with bow on top of tissue paper at bottom of fan. Immediately place remaining craft stick on opposite side of fan so they line up.

9 Decorate both sides of fan with markers or stickers.

What is the best kind of mail to get in the summer? "Fan mail!"

70

This project sponsored by: Fiskars®: Paper Edgers, Scissors

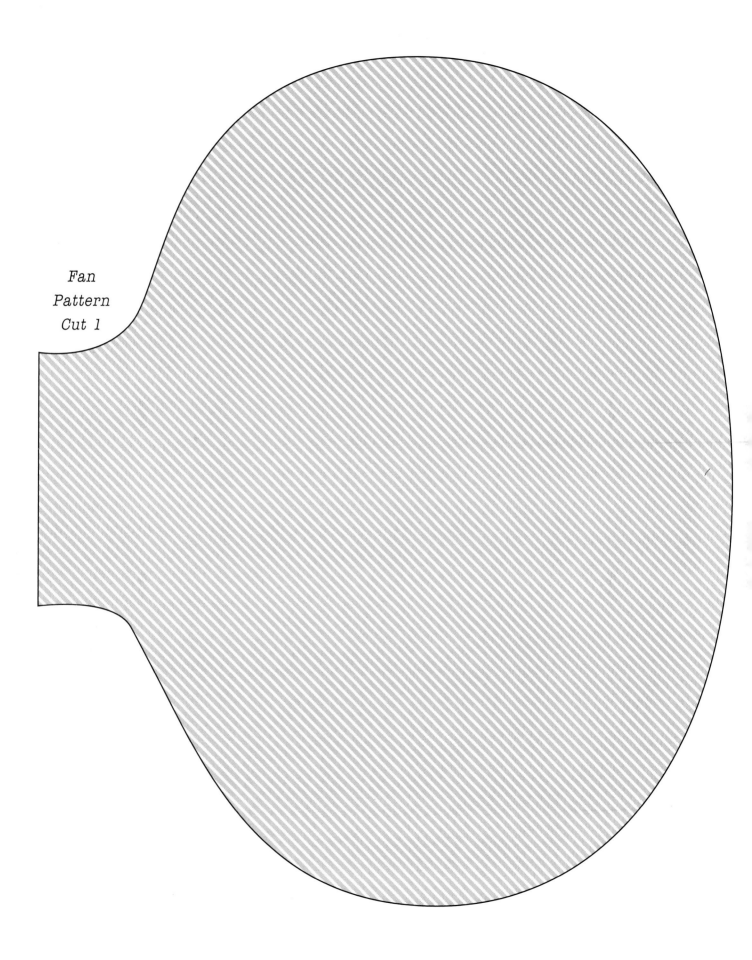

Fan
Pattern
Cut 1

72

plastic plate garden stakes

by CHERYL BALL

Artwork by Heidi Hansen

YOU WILL NEED

To make one garden stake:

- Colored plastic plates:
  (1) 4"-dia.
  (1) 8"-dia.
  (1) 12"-dia.
- Double-sided tape
- Drill with $^1/_8$" bit
- Green acrylic paint
- Green soft-foam sheeting, $^1/_{16}$" thick
- Hammer and nail
- Paintbrush
- Pinking shears
- 24-gauge Plastic-coated wires, any color:
  (1) 18" long
  (1) 24" long
- Scissors
- $^3/_4$"-dia. Wooden dowel, 30" long

1 Cut each plate into separate layers of petals —a different color for each layer is preferable. Equally divide plate into number of petals desired and cut in approximately 4" from outside edge, leaving a minimum of a 2"-diameter circle in center of each layer. If desired, largest plate can be left uncut.

2 Carefully round ends of each petal and, if desired, use pinking shears to trim edges.

Photo on page 74

3 Bend every other petal upward to add dimension.

4 To make the flower, layer petals and hold in place with double-sided tape.

5 Paint dowel with green.

6 Drill two holes, 1" apart, through dowel positioned approximately 4" from one end.

7 Using hammer and nail, make corresponding holes in center of layers of petals.

8 To secure flower to dowel, align holes in petals and dowel and carefully thread 18" length of wire through holes, front to back and back to front. Twist ends in front of flower leaving enough at each end to twist around wire bow.

73

This project sponsored by: Darice®: Foamies™; Delta Ceramcoat®: Acrylic
Paint; Fiskars®: Hand Drill, Pinking Shears, Scissors

9 Bend 24" length of wire into several loops to create a "bow". Twist ends of 18" length of wire at center of bow and curl all ends.

10 Transfer Leaf Pattern at right onto soft-foam sheeting two times.

11 Cut out leaves. Carefully cut out holes in bottom of leaves.

12 Slide leaves onto dowel and position as desired.

"Praise the young and they will blossom."

—Irish proverb

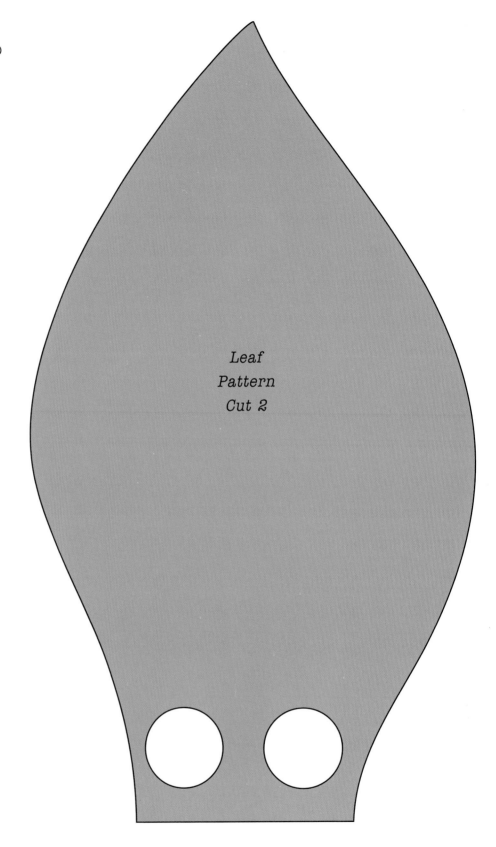

Leaf Pattern Cut 2

dried bean and seed frames

by CHERYL BALL

Artwork by Lance McDonald

YOU WILL NEED

To make three frames:

- Acrylic paints:
  Blue
  Bright pink
  Dark lavender
  Green
  Light green
  Orange
  Pink
  Red
  White
  Yellow
- Craft glue
- Dried beans
  and seeds:
  Kidney beans
  Navy beans
  Pumpkin seeds
- Gloss varnish
- Paintbrush
- (3) Pop-top lids
- Sandpaper
- White gel pen
- (3) Wooden frames,
  5" wide x 7" high

1 Sand frames until smooth. Blow off excess dust.

2 Paint one frame with red, one frame with blue, and one frame with dark lavender.

3 Paint the dried beans and seeds with bright pink, green, light green, orange, pink, white, and yellow as desired.

4 Apply a coat of varnish over frames, beans, and seeds.

5 Glue beans and seeds onto frames.

6 Using the end of the paintbrush handle, paint dots on blue frame with white.

7 Draw wavy lines around outside and inside edges of dark lavender frame with a white gel pen. Randomly add dots on frame and personalize as desired.

8 To make the hangers, glue one pop-top lid to back of each frame.

What did the picture tell the wall?
"First they frame me. Then they hang me!"

This project sponsored by: Delta Ceramcoat® Acrylic Paints, Exterior/Interior Gloss Varnish

77

alien pencil toppers

by CAROL DACE

Artwork by Landon Sexton

YOU WILL NEED

To make one pencil topper:

- Chenille stem, 4" long:
  (1) Green, 6mm
- Cotton swabs
- Craft glue
- 25mm Ornamental plastic toothpicks:
  (4) Any color
  (2) Black
- Pencil
- Pink powder blush
- (2) 1"-dia. Plastic-foam balls
- Powder eye shadow, any color
- Satin ribbons, any color

1 To make the body, push one plastic-foam ball onto eraser-end of pencil, then remove ball.

2 Using a cotton swab, rub eye shadow over body.

3 To make rosy cheeks, use a clean cotton swab to rub blush on each side of remaining ball (head).

4 Using cotton swab with eye shadow on it, rub eye shadow over remaining areas of head.

5 To make eyes, dip ends of two black toothpicks in glue and push into head.

6 To make antennae, dip ends of two colored toothpicks in glue and push into top of head.

7 To make the neck, wrap chenille stem around pencil three times. Remove coiled chenille stem from pencil and straighten each end. Dip ends of chenille stem in glue and push one end into bottom of head and other end into top of body.

8 Dip eraser-end of pencil in glue and insert into hole in bottom of body.

9 To make arms, dip ends of two remaining colored toothpicks in glue and push into sides of body.

10 Tie ribbons around aliens as desired.

How do you get a baby alien to sleep? "You rocket!"

78

This project sponsored by: Darice®: Chenille Stem; Dow Styrofoam®: Plastic Foam

school magnets

by CHERYL BALL

Artwork by Chad Willson

YOU WILL NEED

- Acrylic paints:
  Black
  Brown
  Green
  Orange
  Red
  Silver
  White
  Yellow
- Black medium-tip marker
- Compressed sponge sheeting
- Cotton swab
- Gloss varnish
- Paintbrush
- Scissors
- White magnetic sheeting
- Wooden craft pick

1 Transfer Apple and Leaf Patterns from page 82 onto compressed sponge sheeting.

2 Cut out apple and leaf. Place shapes in water to "plump up," then wring out excess water.

3 Dip apple sponge into red paint and leaf sponge into green. Carefully press onto magnetic sheeting to transfer images.

4 Paint apple stem with brown.

5 Dip a cotton swab into white. Add a highlight on right side of apple.

6 Transfer Pencil, Ruler, and Photo Frame Patterns onto magnetic sheeting.

7 Paint pencil eraser with orange, metal crimp on pencil with silver, body of pencil and ruler with yellow, sharpened lead on pencil with black, and photo frame with red.

8 Dip cotton swab into white. Add a highlight on top of pencil eraser. Randomly add dots on photo frame.

9 Draw details on apple, leaf, pencil, ruler, and photo frame with a marker as shown on patterns and personalize as desired.

10 To make hearts on the half-inch marks on ruler, dip the point of a craft pick into red paint. Make two small dots, side by side, dragging each dot down into a point (heart).

11 Apply a coat of varnish over apple, pencil, ruler, and photo frame magnets.

12 Cut out magnets.

This project sponsored by: Darice®: Compressed Sponge, Magnetic Sheeting; Delta Ceramcoat®: Acrylic Paints, Exterior/Interior Gloss Varnish; Fiskars®: Scissors

*Photo
Frame
Pattern
Cut 1*

*Ruler
Pattern
Cut 1*

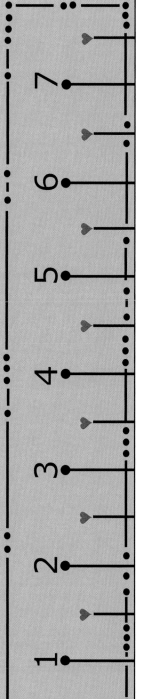

7

6

5

4

3

2

1

*Leaf
Pattern
Cut 1*

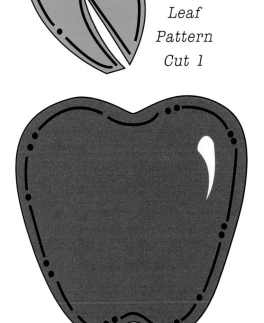

*Apple Pattern
Cut 1 Sponge
Cut 1 Magnet*

*Pencil
Pattern
Cut 1*

back-to-school beauty

by JULIE McGUFFEE

YOU WILL NEED

- Black extrafine-tip marker
- Black wood-craft marker
- Cotton swab
- Craft glue
- Fabric scrap
- Fabric strip, 3" wide x 9" long
- Natural jute:
  (1) 9" long
  (1) 12" long
- Pink powder blush
- Pinking shears
- Sewing needle
- Thread
- Wooden beads:
  (2) $1/2$"-dia. Oval
  (23) $1/4$"-dia. Round
  (1) 1"-dia. Round

1 To make shoes, color oval beads with black wood-craft marker.

2 Tie a knot at center of 12" length of jute. String one shoe, then seven $1/4$"-diameter beads (legs) onto each side of knot as shown in Diagram A below. Tie ends together in an overhand knot up against last beads.

3 String remaining nine $1/4$"-diameter beads (arms) onto 9" length of jute. Center beads on jute, then tie ends together in an overhand knot up against last beads as shown in Diagram B below.

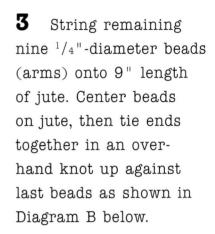

Diagram B

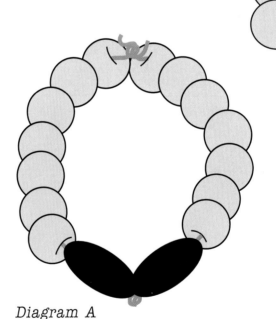

Diagram A

Photo on page 84

This project sponsored by: Darice®: Wood Beads

4 Hold the four ends of jute together and thread through hole in 1"-diameter bead (head) as shown in Diagram C at right.

5 To make hair, separate jute strands, then glue to sides of head.

6 Using pinking shears, trim fabric strip along bottom edge.

7 To make the dress, use a sewing needle and thread to gather-stitch top edge of fabric strip as shown in Diagram D below.

8 Pull dress gathers tightly around base of head, keeping arms on outside and legs on inside and tie off.

9 Stitch back edges together.

10 To make rosy cheeks, use a cotton swab to rub blush on each side of head as shown in Diagram C.

11 Make a dot for each eye and draw a mouth with an extra-fine-tip marker.

12 Tie fabric scrap into a bow and glue it to top of head.

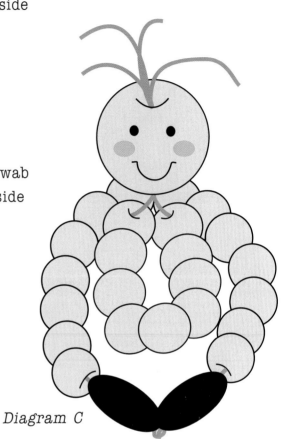

Diagram C

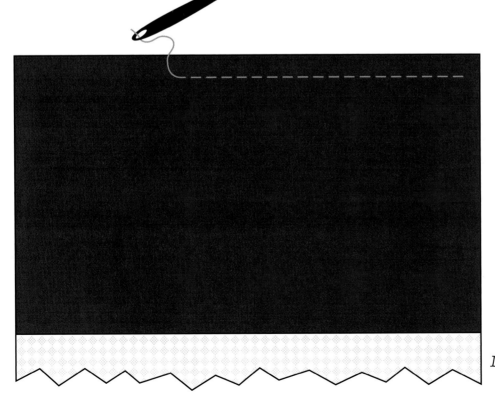

Diagram D

sport magnets

by DIMPLES MUCHERINO

Artwork by Landon Sexton

1 Paint 1^1/$_2$"-diameter disk (baseball) with cream, one 2^1/$_2$"-diameter disk (basketball) with brown, and one 2^1/$_2$"-diameter disk (soccer ball) with white.

2 Paint small star with white, medium star with blue, and large star with red.

3 Draw curved lines on baseball with a black fine-tip marker as shown in Diagram A at right. Draw "stitches" with a red marker.

4 Draw lines on basketball with a black medium-tip marker as shown in Diagram B at right.

YOU WILL NEED

To make one baseball, one basketball, and one soccer ball:

- Acrylic paints:
  Blue
  Brown
  Cream
  Red
  White
- Adhesive-backed magnetic strip, 2^1/$_2$" long
- Black medium-tip marker
- Craft glue
- Felt strips, ^{3}/$_4$" wide x 3" long:
  (1) Blue
  (1) Red

- Fine-tip markers:
  Black
  Red
- Paintbrush
- Ruler
- Scissors
- Wooden disks:
  (1) 1^1/$_2$" dia. x ^{1}/$_4$" thick
  (2) 2^1/$_2$" dia. x ^{1}/$_2$" thick
- Wooden stars:
  (1) Large, flat
  (1) Medium, flat
  (1) Small, flat

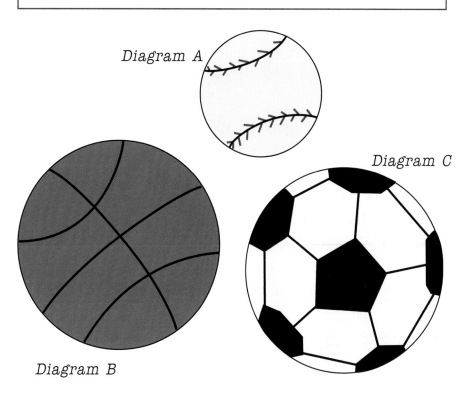

Diagram A

Diagram C

Diagram B

5 Draw pentagon in center of soccer ball as shown in Diagram C on page 86 with the black medium-tip marker. Draw partial pentagons around outsides edges of soccer ball. Draw lines that connect pentagon and partial pentagons.

6 Write #1 on white star with the black fine-tip marker.

7 Glue white star to front of blue star, blue star to front of red star, and red star to front of basketball.

8 Glue felt strips to back of soccer ball.

9 Cut magnetic strip into one $1/2$" length and two 1" lengths.

10 Remove backing from $1/2$" length of magnetic strip and adhere it to back of baseball. Remove backing from 1" lengths of magnetic strip and adhere to backs of basketball and soccer ball.

This project sponsored by: Delta Ceramcoat®: Acrylic Paints; Fiskars®: Scissors; Forster®: Craft Disks, Woodsies™

dancing leaves

by CAROL DACE

Artwork by Kaela Eddy

YOU WILL NEED

- Assorted leaf dies and die cut machine (or leaf patterns and scissors)
- Ballpoint pens: Black Red
- Cluster of silk leaves, autumn colors
- Craft glue
- $1/8$" Hole punch
- (4) Monofilament, 6" long
- (4) Natural raffia strands
- 1"-wide Orange ribbon, 18" long
- Scissors
- Soft-foam sheeting, $1/16$" thick: Brown Orange Red
- Tiny miscellaneous items for faces
- Yellow wire coat hanger

1 Bend a coat hanger and set aside.

2 Cut out leaves using leaf dies and die cut machine, or transfer Leaf 1 Pattern from page 90 onto orange soft-foam sheeting, Leaf 2 Pattern onto red, and Leaf 3 Pattern onto brown and cut out using scissors.

3 Punch one hole in end of each leaf stem.

4 Draw veins on leaves with a black ballpoint pen as shown on patterns. Draw dashed lines around orange leaf.

5 To make faces on leaves, glue tiny miscellaneous items (like pompoms, wiggle eyes, and buttons) in place.

6 Draw eyebrows, eyelashes, freckles, and mouths on leaves with black and red ballpoint pens as desired.

7 Using one length of monofilament, tie silk leaves to top of coat hanger.

8 Wrap raffia and ribbon around top of coat hanger and tie into bows.

9 Tie one end of remaining lengths of monofilament to holes in leaf stems and the other ends to coat hanger.

This project sponsored by: Darice®: Foamies™, Pom-poms, Raffia,
Wiggle Eyes; Ellison: Die Cut Machine; Fiskars®: Hole Punch, Scissors

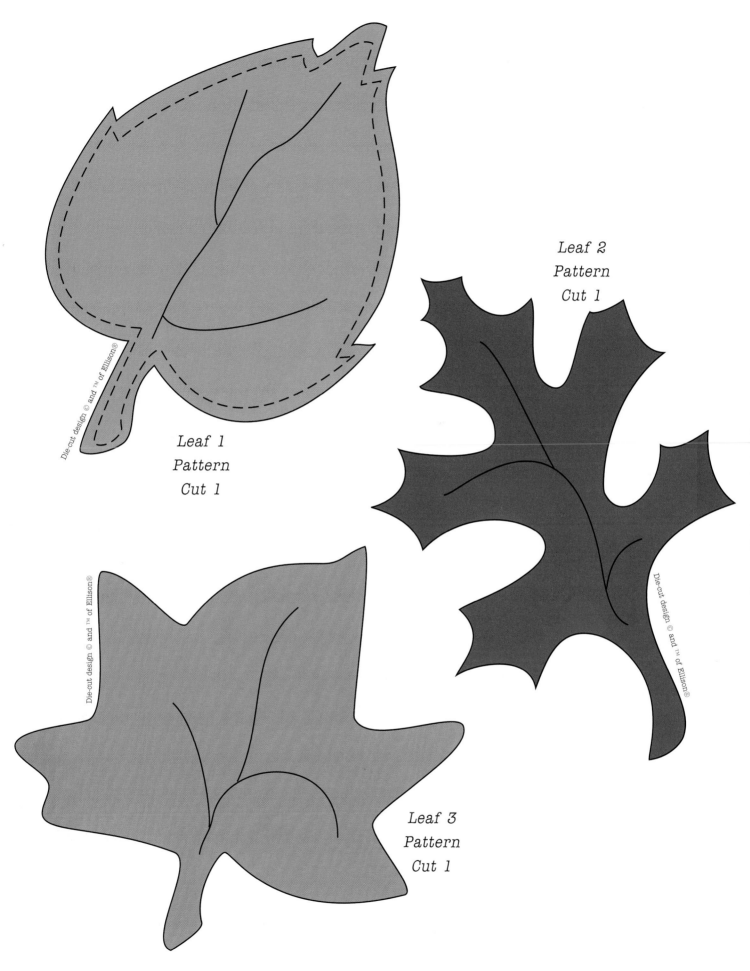

Leaf 1
Pattern
Cut 1

Leaf 2
Pattern
Cut 1

Leaf 3
Pattern
Cut 1

Die-cut design © and ™ of Ellison®

Die-cut design © and ™ of Ellison®

Die-cut design © and ™ of Ellison®

90

frightful friend
wind sock

by JULIE McGUFFEE

Artwork by Landon Sexton

YOU WILL NEED

- Black medium-tip marker
- Craft glue
- Natural jute, 12" long
- Scissors
- Soft-foam sheeting, 1/16" thick:
  Black
  White
- White plastic trash bag
- Wire coat hanger

Instructions begin on page 92

This project sponsored by: Darice®: Foamies™; Fiskars®: Scissors

1 Transfer Head Pattern from page 93 onto white soft-foam sheeting two times and Eye Pattern onto black two times.

2 Cut out heads and eyes.

3 To make the ghost, glue eyes on one head.

4 Draw eyebrows and mouth on ghost with a marker as shown on pattern.

5 Cut a small hole at bottom center of trash bag. Slide a coat hanger into trash bag, pushing the "hook" out through opening.

6 Starting at left, cut 3"-wide streamers along bottom edge of trash bag, up to bottom of coat hanger as shown in Diagram A at right.

7 To make the loop for hanging, place ends of jute together and tie a knot. Place loop around "hook" on coat hanger.

8 Glue the heads together with coat hanger and loop for hanging in between the two layers.

Diagram A

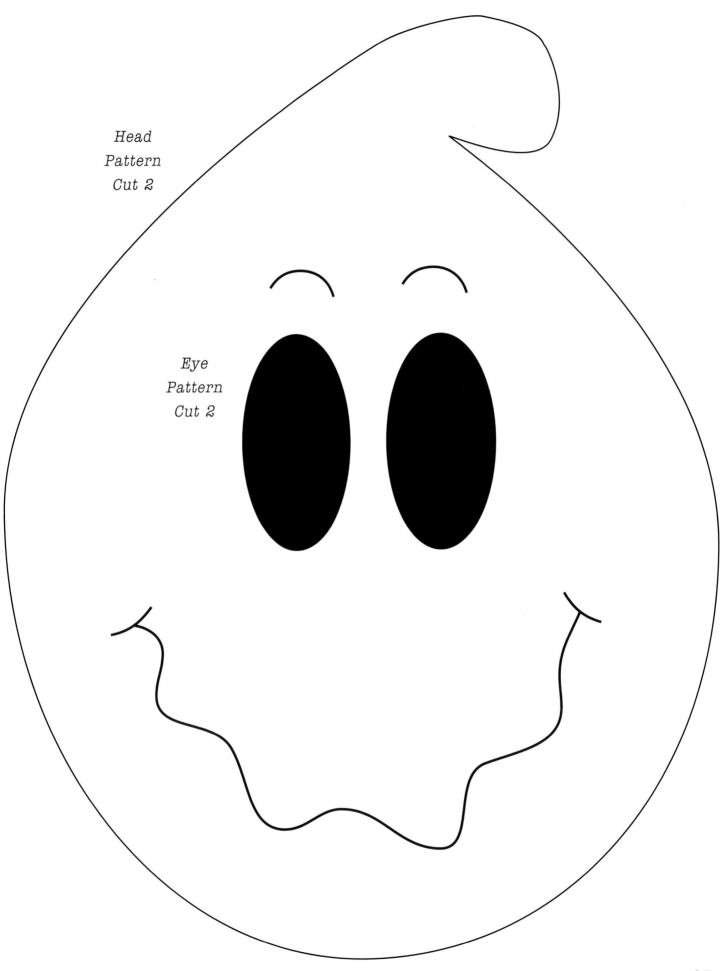

Head
Pattern
Cut 2

Eye
Pattern
Cut 2

spooky spider gloves

by JULIE McGUFFEE

Artwork by Hollie Odekirk

YOU WILL NEED

- Black fabric gardening gloves
- Black medium-tip marker
- Chenille stems, 10" long: (8) Any color, 6mm
- Craft glue
- 3"-dia. Plastic-foam ball
- Scissors
- Straight pin
- White soft-foam sheeting, ¹/₁₆" thick

1 Place one chenille stem inside each finger of both gloves as shown in Diagram A below.

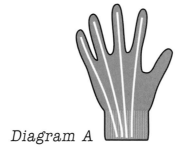

Diagram A

2 Trim ends of each chenille stem even with bottom of cuffs.

3 Pull cuff of one glove around plastic-foam ball as shown in Diagram B below, keeping the four chenille stems together underneath ball.

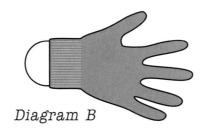

Diagram B

4 Pull cuff of remaining glove over cuff of glove containing ball as shown in Diagram C

below, keeping the eight chenille stems together underneath ball. Make certain both thumbs are on same side of ball.

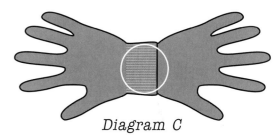

Diagram C

5 Overlap thumbs in front of cuff; glue together, then to cuff. Pin thumbs in place. Let glue dry, then remove straight pin.

6 To make the eyes, cut two nickle-sized circles from soft-foam sheeting. Draw pupils on lower half of eyes with a marker.

7 Glue eyes to cuff above thumbs.

8 To shape the spider's legs, bend chenille stems inside fingers of gloves.

94

This project sponsored by: Darice®: Chenille Stems, Foamies™; Dow Styrofoam®: Plastic Foam

pumpkin wind sock

by CHERYL BALL

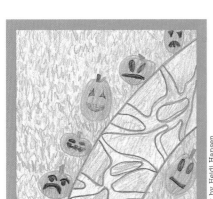

Artwork by Heidi Hansen

YOU WILL NEED

- Acrylic paints:
  Green
  Lavender
  Orange
  Yellow
- Black medium-tip marker
- Craft glue
- Orange lunch sack
- Orange shoelace, 30" long
- Paintbrush
- Pencil
- Pinking shears
- Purple flat-fold crepe paper
- Ruler
- Scissors
- White poster board
- Yellow fabric strip, 1 1/2" wide x 24" long

This project sponsored by: Bemiss-Jason: Spectra® Art Crepe™; Delta Ceramcoat®: Acrylic Paints; Fiskars®: Pinking Shears, Scissors; Sakura of America: Identipen™

1 Cut poster board into four 8" squares.

2 Paint one square with green, one square with lavender, one square with orange, and one square with yellow.

3 Transfer the Eye 1 Pattern at right onto yellow piece of poster board two times, Eye 2 Pattern onto orange two times, Eye 3 and Cheek Patterns onto lavender two times, Nose Pattern onto orange one time, and Leaf Pattern onto green six times.

4 Cut out eyes, nose, cheeks, and leaves.

5 Draw details on cutouts with a marker as shown on patterns.

6 To make the pumpkin, glue cutouts on sack. The eye should be layered as shown in Diagram A at right. The open end of sack should be facing down.

7 Draw mouth and vertical lines on pumpkin with the marker.

8 Using pinking shears, cut crepe paper into 1¹/₂" wavy strips. Unfold strips and cut into ten 18" streamers.

9 Glue streamers around inside of open end of sack and three remaining leaves to streamers as desired.

10 Using pinking shears, trim the fabric strip. Using scissors, cut a "V" at ends of fabric strip. With sack completely open, tie fabric strip around it and glue in place.

11 Using the point of a sharpened pencil, make one small hole on each side at top of sack.

12 To make the loop for hanging, carefully thread shoelace through holes and tie ends in a knot.

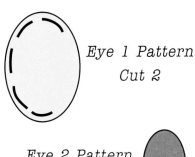

*Eye 1 Pattern
Cut 2*

*Eye 2 Pattern
Cut 2*

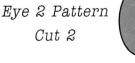

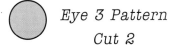

*Eye 3 Pattern
Cut 2*

*Nose
Pattern
Cut 1*

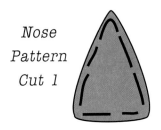

*Cheek
Pattern
Cut 2*

*Leaf
Pattern
Cut 6*

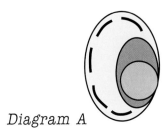

Diagram A

candy cones

by JULIE McGUFFEE

Artwork by Jaime Schultz

YOU WILL NEED

To make one candy cone:

- Candy
- Craft glue
- 10"-dia. Disposable plate
- 1/8" Hole punch
- Pencil
- Ruler
- 1/4"-wide Satin ribbon, any color: 12" long
- Scissors
- Stickers
- Tape
- Tissue paper, any color
- Waffle paper, any color

1 Cut disposable plate in half. Using one half as a pattern, trace onto waffle paper and cut out.

2 Mark center of straight edge with a pencil. Using mark as a guide, roll waffle paper into a cone as shown in Diagram A below. Tape in place.

Diagram A

3 Cut tissue paper into one 10"-wide by 20"-long strip, then fold in half lengthwise to measure 5"-wide. Make a firm crease, then accordion-fold the entire length of tissue paper as shown in Diagram B at right.

4 Place accordion-folded tissue paper inside cone, with folded edge at top, and spread out so tissue paper goes completely around top inside edges of cone. Glue in place.

5 Punch one hole on opposite sides of cone.

6 To make the handle, thread ribbon through each hole and tie in an overhand knot.

7 Decorate cone with stickers and fill with candy.

Diagram B

This project sponsored by: Bemiss-Jason: Tissue Paper, Waffle Paper;
Fiskars®: Hole Punch, Scissors

halloween necklace

by **BARB ZIMMERMAN**

Artwork by Max Butler

1 Paint two spools with black and two spools with orange.

2 Using the point of a sharpened pencil, make one small hole through center of plastic-foam ball.

3 To make the ghost, place ball in center of fabric square, positioning holes where ears would be. Wrap fabric around it and secure with a rubber band at neck.

4 Snip holes in fabric on each side of ghost's head to line up with hole through ball.

YOU WILL NEED

- Acrylic paints:
  Black
  Orange
- Black fine-tip marker
- Black leather cord, 24" long
- Craft glue
- Paintbrush
- Pencil
- $1^1/_2$"-dia. Plastic-foam ball
- Rubber band
- Satin ribbons:
  $^1/_4$"-wide Black, 12" long
  $^1/_8$"-wide Orange, 12" long
- Scissors
- White cotton fabric, 10" square
- White fine-tip opaque marker
- (2) Wiggle eyes, 7mm
- (4) $^3/_4$"-dia. Wooden spools

5 Wrap ribbons around ghost's neck, hiding the rubber band, and tie into a bow.

6 Glue eyes in place.

7 Draw a jack-o-lantern face on each orange spool with a black marker.

8 Draw a series of eyes on each black spool with a white marker. Draw pupils in each eye with the black marker.

9 Thread one black spool, one orange spool, the ghost, one orange spool, and one black spool onto leather cord. Adjust cord to desired length and tie ends together in a knot.

This project sponsored by: Darice®: Leather Cord, Wiggle Eyes, Wooden
Spools; Delta Ceramcoat®: Acrylic Paints; Dow Styrofoam®: Plastic Foam

vampire bat doorknob hanger

by **MARY AYRES**

Artwork by Matthew Romney

YOU WILL NEED

- Black medium-tip marker
- Craft glue
- Scissors
- Soft-foam sheeting, 1/16" thick:
  Black
  Purple
  White
- (2) Wiggle eyes, 12mm

1 Transfer Bat Pattern from page 104 onto purple soft-foam sheeting one time, Fang Pattern from below onto white two times, and Ear, Wing 1, Wing 2, and Wing 3 Patterns onto black two times.

2 Cut out bat, fangs, ears, and wings. Carefully cut out hole in center of bat.

3 Draw face on bat with a marker as shown on pattern.

4 Glue eyes in place.

5 Glue cutouts on bat.

6 Draw an outline around outside edges of bat, around hole in center of bat, and between each section of wings with the marker.

Fang
Pattern
Cut 2

Ear
Pattern
Cut 2

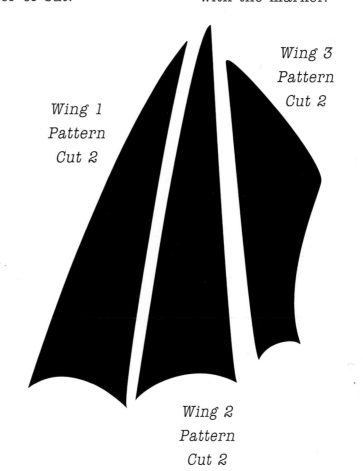

Wing 1
Pattern
Cut 2

Wing 3
Pattern
Cut 2

Wing 2
Pattern
Cut 2

This project sponsored by: Darice®: Foamies™, Wiggle Eyes; Fiskars®: Scissors

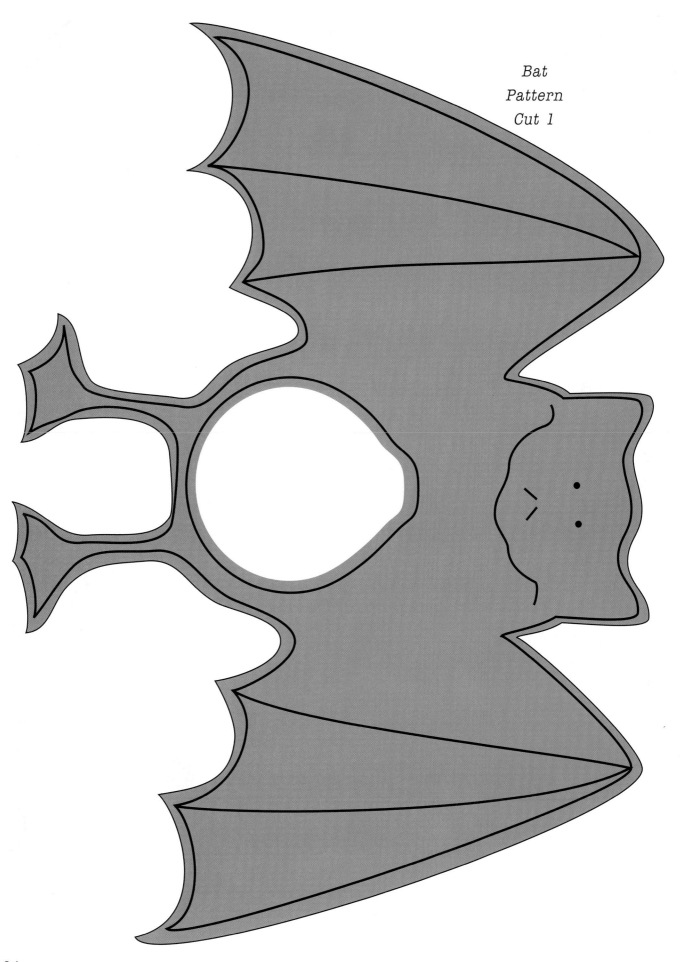

Bat
Pattern
Cut 1

104

abstract star pin

by JULIE McGUFFEE

Artwork by Travis Grant

YOU WILL NEED

- Adhesive-backed pin back
- Craft glue
- $1/16$" Hole punch
- (3) Pearl-white buttons
- Silver glitter glue pen
- Thin gold wires
- Toothpick
- Wooden stars:
  (1) Medium, flat
  (1) Small, flat
- Yellow wood-craft marker

1 Color stars with yellow wood-craft marker.

2 Punch one hole in each star. To punch holes in thin wood, punch where wood grain is running up and down and not across.

3 Glue small star on top of medium star, then randomly wrap both stars with one length of wire. Curl second length of wire by wrapping around a toothpick. Thread one end of second wire through holes in small star and one button, then thread other end through hole in medium star and one button. Glue one button to star.

4 Add dots on stars with a glitter glue pen.

5 Remove backing from pin back and adhere to back of medium star.

This project sponsored by: Fiskars®: Hole Punch; Forster®: Woodsies™; Toner Plastics™: Fun Wire™

quilted-wood magnets

by BRENDA SPITZER

Artwork by Chaz Smith

YOU WILL NEED

To make one magnet:

- Adhesive-backed magnetic strip, 1" long
- Chisel-tip opaque markers: Assorted colors
- Fine-tip markers: Assorted colors
- Wood glue
- Wooden shapes: Assorted wood-quilting shapes (1) 1¹/₂" Square

1 Color the assorted wood-quilting shapes with colored chisel-tip markers.

2 Glue shapes on top of 1¹/₂" square as desired.

3 Draw details on shapes with colored fine-tip markers.

4 Remove backing from magnetic strip and adhere to back of 1¹/₂" square.

A Rainy-Day Tea Party

Rain, rain, go away,
Come again another day!

· M · E · N · U ·
LEMON DRIZZLE CAKE
CLOUD COOKIES
MUD PIES
RAINY-DAY TEA

It's raining! It's pouring! You press your nose to the window
and watch the raindrops zigzag down the pane. It looks as if the
rain will never stop. But don't be glum. Perk up a rainy day with
a tea party!

For decorations, you can hang lightning bolts right over the
table. But the only clouds at this party will be the ones you eat
on—cloud place mats—and the ones you eat up—cloud cookies.
Rain, rain, don't go away!

LEMON DRIZZLE CAKE

You will need:
A juicer
1 large lemon

1 tablespoons sugar
1 pound cake

17

This project sponsored by: Darice®: Adhesive-backed Magnet Strip; Sakura of
America: Identipen™, Permapaque™ Opaque Pigment Markers

pinecone topiary

by JULIE McGUFFEE

YOU WILL NEED

- Acrylic paints:
  Black
  Gold
  White
- Craft glue
- Craft knife
- 1/2"-wide Gold mesh ribbon, 12" long
- Gray moss
- Paintbrush
- Pinecone, approx. 5" high
- Plastic foam, 2" wide x 1³/₄" high
- Small clay pot, 2¹/₂" dia. x 2¹/₄" high
- Small sponge
- 1/8"-dia. Wooden dowel, 2" long
- 1/2"-dia. Wooden spool

1 Paint clay pot with black.

2 Dip sponge into gold and lightly sponge pot.

3 Wash gold from sponge and dip into white. Sponge tips of pinecone.

4 Assemble the topiary as shown in Diagram A at right. To do this, glue spool to base of pinecone. If necessary, remove a few petals from pinecone to make base as flat as possible. Place pinecone upside down in pot. Let glue dry, then remove pinecone.

5 Using a craft knife, carefully trim plastic foam to fit inside pot.

6 Glue plastic foam into pot and cover top with moss.

7 Glue dowel into hole in spool.

8 Push dowel into plastic foam inside pot.

9 Wrap ribbon around rim of pot and tie into a bow.

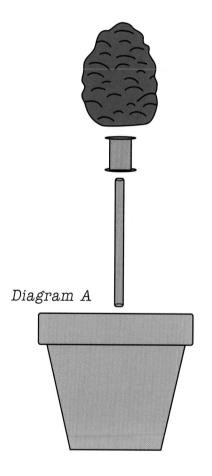

Diagram A

108

This project sponsored by: Darice®: Wooden Spool; Delta Ceramcoat®:
Acrylic Paints; Dow Styrofoam®: Plastic Foam

snowman family ornaments

by JEAN KIEVLAN

Artwork by Lance McDonald

YOU WILL NEED

- Acrylic paints:
  Light blue
  Orange
  White
- Black fine-tip marker
- Chenille stems, 4" long:
  (1) Blue, 6mm
  (1) Red, 6mm
- Cotton swab
- Craft glue
- Felt strips, 3/4" wide x 8" long:
  (1) Blue
  (2) Green
  (2) Red
- (5) Gold cords or ribbons, 4" long
- Paintbrush
- Pink powder blush
- 3/8" Pom-poms:
  (2) Light green
  (2) Red
- Scissors
- Small sponge
- (5) 1/4" Wooden button plugs
- Wooden circles:
  (3) 1 3/4" dia. x 1/4" thick
  (2) 2 1/2" dia. x 1/4" thick

1 To make snowmen, paint circles with white.

2 Dip sponge into light blue and lightly sponge around outside edges of snowmen.

3 To make the noses, paint button plugs with orange.

4 Glue one nose in center of each snowman.

5 To make rosy cheeks, use a cotton swab to rub blush on each side of noses.

6 Draw a face on each snowman with a marker.

7 To make scarves, cut fringe along ends of each felt strip.

8 Glue scarves around bottoms of snowmen (necks).

9 To make ear muffs for the two large snowmen, glue one chenille stem along contour of each head. Glue one pom-pom at each end of chenille stems.

10 To make the loops for hanging, place ends of each length of cord together and tie a knot.

11 Glue one loop to back of each snowman.

This project sponsored by: Darice®: Chenille Stems, Cord, Felt, Pom-poms;
Delta Ceramcoat®: Acrylic Paints; Fiskars®: Scissors

snowman wind sock

by CHERYL BALL

Artwork by Daniel Savage

YOU WILL NEED

- Acrylic paints:
  Black
  Green
  Orange
  Pink
  Red
  Yellow
- Blue fabric strip,
  2" wide x 24" long
- Craft glue
- Light blue flat-fold
  crepe paper
- Medium-tip markers:
  Black
  Blue

- Paintbrush
- Pencil
- Pinking shears
- Ruler
- Scissors
- White fine-tip
  opaque marker
- White lunch sack
- White poster board
- White shoelace,
  30" long

1 Cut poster board into seven 8" squares.

2 Paint one square with black, one square with green, one square with orange, one square with pink, one square with red, and one square with yellow. One square will be left unpainted.

3 Transfer the Eye Pattern from page 114 onto black piece of poster board two times, Nose Pattern onto orange one time, Cheek Pattern onto pink two times, Button Pattern onto yellow one time, Holly Leaf Pattern onto green three times, and Holly Berry Pattern onto red three times. Transfer Snowflake 1 Pattern one time and Snowflake 2 Pattern two times onto unpainted piece of poster board.

4 Cut out eyes, nose, cheeks, button, leaves, berries, and snowflakes. Using pinking shears, trim each snowflake.

5 Draw details on cutouts with a black marker as shown on patterns. Add a tiny dot to upper right corners of each pupil with a white marker. Draw snowflakes with a blue marker.

6 To make the snowman, glue cutouts on sack. The open end of sack should be facing down.

This project sponsored by: Bemiss-Jason: Spectra® Art Crepe™;
Delta Ceramcoat®: Acrylic Paints; Fiskars®: Pinking Shears, Scissors

7 Draw mouth on snowman with the black marker.

8 Using pinking shears, cut crepe paper into 1¹/₂" wavy strips. Unfold strips and cut into nine 20" streamers.

9 Glue streamers around inside of open end of sack and snow-flakes to three streamers as desired.

10 Using pinking shears, trim the fabric strip. Using scissors, cut fringe along ends of fabric strip. With sack completely open, tie fabric strip around it and glue in place.

11 Using the point of a sharpened pencil, make one small hole on each side at top of sack.

12 To make the loop for hanging, carefully thread shoelace through holes and tie ends in a knot.

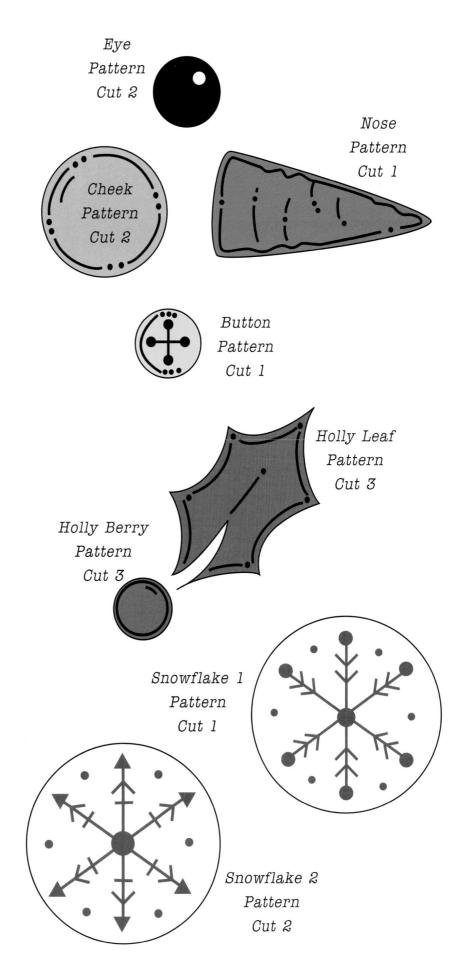

Eye Pattern Cut 2

Nose Pattern Cut 1

Cheek Pattern Cut 2

Button Pattern Cut 1

Holly Leaf Pattern Cut 3

Holly Berry Pattern Cut 3

Snowflake 1 Pattern Cut 1

Snowflake 2 Pattern Cut 2

114

paint-roller penguin

by DIMPLES MUCHERINO

Artwork by Matthew Romney

*Instructions
begin on page 116*

*What's
black and
white
and red
all over?
"A penguin
with a
sunburn!"*

This project sponsored by: Darice®: Felt, Jingle Bell, Pony Beads; Delta Ceramcoat®: Acrylic Paints; Fiskars®: Scissors; Forster®: Craft Spoons, Craft Sticks, Woodsies™

- Acrylic paints:
  Black
  Dark green
  Red
  Yellow
- Black felt,
  $6^1/_2$" wide x
  $8^3/_4$" long
- Black fine-tip
  marker
- Craft glue
- Evergreen sprig,
  5" long
- Holly berry stem,
  3" long
- $^1/_2$" Jingle bell
- Natural jute,
  18" long
- Old sock:
  child's size,
  any color
- Paintbrush
- Scissors
- (2) Turquoise
  opaque pony beads
- White disposable
  paint roller
- (2) Wooden craft
  spoons
- (2) Wooden jumbo
  craft sticks
- Wooden shapes:
  (1) Large
     teardrop, flat
  (1) Small star, flat

1 Paint teardrop (beak) with yellow, star with dark green, craft spoons (wings) with black, and craft sticks (skis) with red.

2 Draw nostrils and dashed lines around beak and skis with a marker as shown in Diagram A below.

Diagram A

3 Transfer Coat Pattern from page 117 onto felt. Make certain to place on fold.

4 Cut out coat.

5 Keeping top and bottom edges even, place paint roller on coat. Apply glue along inside, left front edge and glue to paint roller. Repeat on right side.

6 To make the face, glue beads (eyes) and beak to paint roller.

7 Glue wings to sides of coat as shown on pattern.

8 Glue skis in position at bottom of paint roller.

9 Wrap jute around neck and tie into a bow. Glue bell to center of bow.

10 To make the hat, cut sock 6" from toe end. Starting at cut end, roll a 2" double cuff and place hat on top of paint roller as shown in Diagram B on page 117.

11 Glue star to front of hat.

12 Glue evergreen sprig to back of one wing. Wrap holly berry stem around evergreen sprig and wing and twist ends together in front.

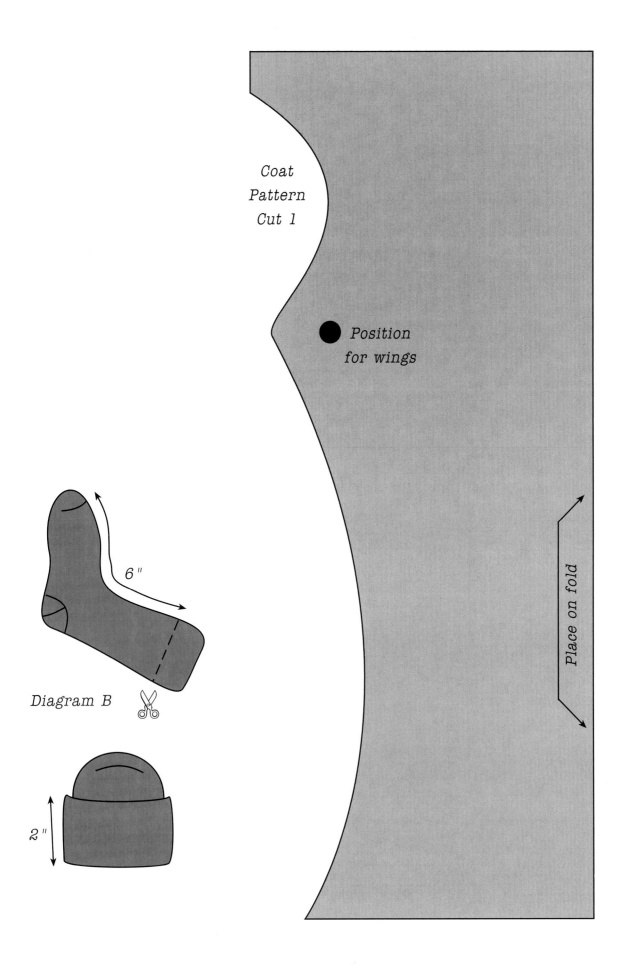

Coat
Pattern
Cut 1

● Position
for wings

Place on fold

6 "

Diagram B

2 "

christmas cat

by **DIMPLES MUCHERINO**

YOU WILL NEED

- Acrylic paints:
  Brown
  Red
  White
- Chenille stems,
  10" long:
  (1) Red, 6mm
  (1) White, 6mm
- Craft glue
- Drill with $1/8$" bit
- Fine-tip markers:
  Black
  Green
- Paintbrush
- (3) Red raffia
  strands
- Wooden craft pick
- Wooden disk,
  $2^1/_2$" dia. x
  $1/_2$" thick
- Wooden shapes:
  (1) Circle, $1^1/_4$"
      dia. x $1/_4$" thick
  (2) Pumpkins, flat
  (2) Teardrops, flat

1 Drill a hole in top of disk as shown in Diagram A below.

Diagram A

2 Paint disk (body), circle (head), and teardrops (ears) with white and pumpkins (paws) with brown.

3 Dry-brush around outside edges of body, at sides of head, and across pointed ends of ears with brown.

4 Draw eyes with a green marker.

5 To make the nose, dip the point of a craft pick into red paint. Make two small dots, side by side, dragging each dot down into a point (heart).

6 Draw whiskers, mouth, and lines on ears and paws with a black marker.

7 Glue ears to back of head, paws to back of body, and back of ears to body.

8 To make the tail, insert both chenille stems into drilled hole. Fold stems in half and twist together. Bend tip of tail to form a "hook" for hanging.

9 Wrap raffia around base of tail and tie into a bow.

What do you call a cat at the beach? "Sandy claws!"

This project sponsored by: Darice®: Chenille Stems, Raffia; Delta
Ceramcoat®: Acrylic Paints; Fiskars®: Hand Drill; Forster®: Craft
Disk, Craft Pick, Woodsies™; Sakura of America: Identipen™

cookie-cutter snowman

by JULIE McGUFFEE

YOU WILL NEED

- Beads:
  (3) Medium black
  (2) Small black
- Black soft-foam sheeting, $1/16$" thick
- Chenille stems, 10" long:
  (1) Black, 6mm
  (1) Red, 12mm
- Craft glue
- Green floral stake
- Large metal snowman cookie cutter
- Plastic-foam sheeting, 1" thick
- Ruler
- Scissors
- Tape
- Toothpick

1 Using a cookie cutter, cut out a snowman shape from plastic-foam sheeting. To do this, place sharp edge of cookie cutter on surface of plastic foam. Gently press with an even amount of pressure until cookie cutter cuts through plastic foam, then carefully remove cookie cutter.

2 To make eyes, push two small beads into head.

3 To make buttons, push three medium beads into body (only two buttons show in photo).

4 To make the top hat, cut one $1^1/2$"-diameter circle and one $3/4$"-wide by 6"-long strip from soft-foam sheeting.

5 Spread glue along one side of soft-foam strip and tightly roll as shown in Diagram A at right. Hold in place with tape. Let glue dry, then remove tape.

6 Glue rolled foam to center of soft-foam circle.

7 Place hat on snowman. Push a toothpick down through center of top hat and into top of head.

8 To make the scarf, wrap red chenille stem around neck. Twist ends together.

9 To make arms, cut black chenille stem in half. Bend one end of each half to look like a twig. Dip opposite ends into glue and push one into each side of body.

10 Push a floral stake into bottom of snowman.

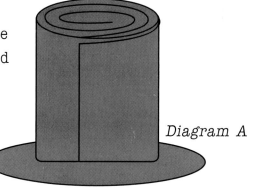

Diagram A

This project sponsored by: Darice®: Beads, Chenille Stems, Foamies™;
Dow Styrofoam®: Plastic Foam; Fiskars®: Scissors

paper doily angels

by JULIE McGUFFEE

Artwork by Kaela Eddy

YOU WILL NEED

To make one angel:

- Black extrafine-tip marker
- Cotton swab
- Craft glue
- Gold heart paper doily, 4"
- Pink powder blush
- Ribbon bow with rose trim, blue or pink

- Scissors
- White paper doily, 6" dia.
- $^1/_8$"-wide White satin ribbon, 6" long
- Wood-craft markers: Flesh Gold
- Wooden circles: $^3/_4$" dia. x $^1/_8$" thick $1^1/_4$" dia. x $^1/_8$" thick

1 To make angel's dress, fold round doily so one edge is $^1/_2$" shorter than the other as shown in Diagram A below. Fold each side to back to form a triangle as shown by dashed lines and glue sides together.

Diagram A

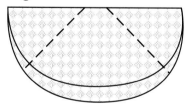

2 Using wood-craft markers, color $1^1/_4$"-diameter circle (halo) with gold and $^3/_4$"-diameter circle (head) with flesh.

3 Pinch top of doily to flatten, then glue dress to back of halo as shown in Diagram B below.

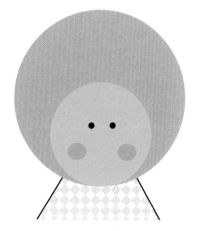

Diagram B

4 To make rosy cheeks, use a cotton swab to rub blush on each side of head.

5 Make a dot for each eye with a black marker.

6 Glue head to halo.

7 Glue ribbon bow to top front of dress.

8 To make wings, cut heart doily in half and glue to back of halo and dress.

9 To make the loop for hanging, glue ends of ribbon to back of halo.

This project sponsored by: Darice®: Wood Parts; Fiskars®: Scissors

foil-embossed greeting card

by JULIE McGUFFEE

Artwork by Tiffany Allen

YOU WILL NEED

To make one card:

- Aluminum foil, 5" square
- Card stock, 5$\frac{1}{2}$" wide x 11" long
- Craft glue
- Decorative-edged scissors: Pinking
- Natural jute
- Pencil

1 Fold length of card stock in half to make a square. Crease it at fold.

2 At center of card, sketch a design. Place jute over the design and glue in place as shown in Diagram A below.

3 Apply glue over card and jute, leaving at least a $\frac{1}{2}$" border away from all edges.

4 Using decorative-edged scissors, trim aluminum foil square. Lay foil on top of jute design and firmly press to achieve embossed effect.

Diagram A

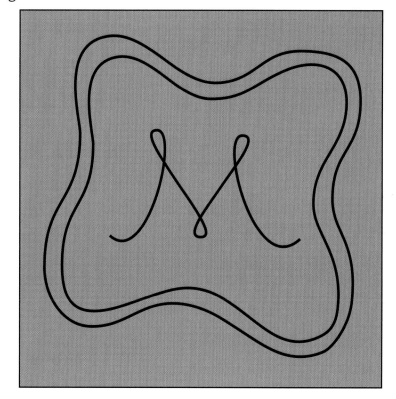

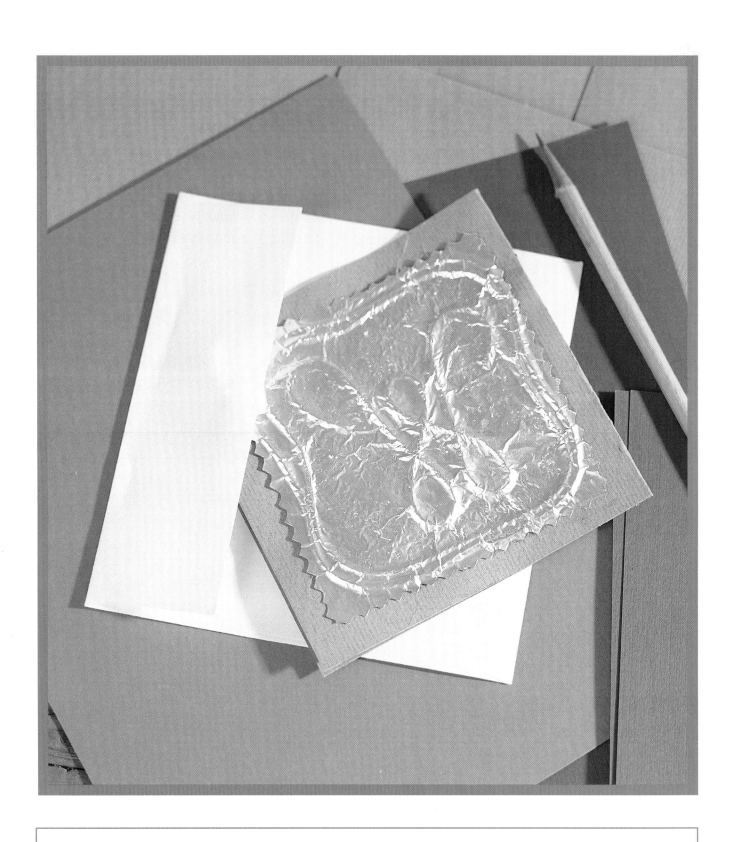

This project sponsored by: Fiskars®: Paper Edgers

acknowledgments

A very special thanks to:
East Layton Elementary
Layton, Utah
Mrs. Amy Algoe's 5th Grade Class
for the artwork used
throughout this publication.

Bemiss-Jason
*Art papers, craft materials,
and tools for creative learning.*

525 Enterprise
P.O. Box 699
Neenah, WI 54957
1-800-544-0093
www.bemiss-jason.com

Darice®
*Providing creative people with craft,
floral, art, and home decorating supplies.*

21160 Drake Road
Strongsville, OH 44136
www.darice.com

Delta Technical Coatings, Inc.
If it's worth doing, it's worth Delta.

2550 Pellissier Place
Whittier, CA 90601-1505
1-800-423-4135
www.deltacrafts.com

The Dow Chemical Company
*Styrofoam® brand products from
The Dow Chemical Company—
a creative favorite for kid's crafts.*

1610 Building
Midland, MI 48674-0001
www.styrofoam-crafts.com

Ellison
*Ellison's die-cutting machines
and die shapes create
easy, imaginative learning projects.*

25862 Commercentre Drive
Lake Forest, CA 92630
1-800-253-2238
www.ellison.com

Fiskars®
At home with innovation™.

2811 W. Stewart Avenue
Wausau, WI 54401
1-715-842-2091
www.fiskars.com

Forster
*Your woodcraft leader
for products and project ideas.*

P. O. Box 657
Wilton, ME 04294
1-800-777-7942
www.diamondbrands.com

Sakura of America
Empower your imagination!

30780 San Clemente Street
Hayward, CA 94544
1-800-776-6257
www.gellyroll.com

Toner Plastics, Inc.™
We sell fun! Camp Hoochee Coochee.

699 Silver Street
Agawan, MA 01001
1-800-723-1792
www.tonerplastics.com

metric conversions

INCHES TO MILLIMETRES AND CENTIMETRES

MM-Millimetres   **CM-Centimetres**

INCHES	MM	CM	INCHES	CM	INCHES	CM
$1/8$	3	0.9	9	22.9	30	76.2
$1/4$	6	0.6	10	25.4	31	78.7
$3/8$	10	1.0	11	27.9	32	81.3
$1/2$	13	1.3	12	30.5	33	83.8
$5/8$	16	1.6	13	33.0	34	86.4
$3/4$	19	1.9	14	35.6	35	88.9
$7/8$	22	2.2	15	38.1	36	91.4
1	25	2.5	16	40.6	37	94.0
$1^{1}/4$	32	3.2	17	43.2	38	96.5
$1^{1}/2$	38	3.8	18	45.7	39	99.1
$1^{3}/4$	44	4.4	19	48.3	40	101.6
2	51	5.1	20	50.8	41	104.1
$2^{1}/2$	64	6.4	21	53.3	42	106.7
3	76	7.6	22	55.9	43	109.2
$3^{1}/2$	89	8.9	23	58.4	44	111.8
4	102	10.2	24	61.0	45	114.3
$4^{1}/2$	114	11.4	25	63.5	46	116.8
5	127	12.7	26	66.0	47	119.4
6	152	15.2	27	68.6	48	121.9
7	178	17.8	28	71.1	49	124.5
8	203	20.3	29	73.7	50	127.0

YARDS TO METRES

YARDS	METRES	YARDS	METRES	YARDS	METRES	YARDS	METRES	YARDS	METRES
$1/8$	0.11	$2^{1}/8$	1.94	$4^{1}/8$	3.77	$6^{1}/8$	5.60	$8^{1}/8$	7.43
$1/4$	0.23	$2^{1}/4$	2.06	$4^{1}/4$	3.89	$6^{1}/4$	5.72	$8^{1}/4$	7.54
$3/8$	0.34	$2^{3}/8$	2.17	$4^{3}/8$	4.00	$6^{3}/8$	5.83	$8^{3}/8$	7.66
$1/2$	0.46	$2^{1}/2$	2.29	$4^{1}/2$	4.11	$6^{1}/2$	5.94	$8^{1}/2$	7.77
$5/8$	0.57	$2^{5}/8$	2.40	$4^{5}/8$	4.23	$6^{5}/8$	6.06	$8^{5}/8$	7.89
$3/4$	0.69	$2^{3}/4$	2.51	$4^{3}/4$	4.34	$6^{3}/4$	6.17	$8^{3}/4$	8.00
$7/8$	0.80	$2^{7}/8$	2.63	$4^{7}/8$	4.46	$6^{7}/8$	6.29	$8^{7}/8$	8.12
1	0.91	3	2.74	5	4.57	7	6.40	9	8.23
$1^{1}/8$	1.03	$3^{1}/8$	2.86	$5^{1}/8$	4.69	$7^{1}/8$	6.52	$9^{1}/8$	8.34
$1^{1}/4$	1.14	$3^{1}/4$	2.97	$5^{1}/4$	4.80	$7^{1}/4$	6.63	$9^{1}/4$	8.46
$1^{3}/8$	1.26	$3^{3}/8$	3.09	$5^{3}/8$	4.91	$7^{3}/8$	6.74	$9^{3}/8$	8.57
$1^{1}/2$	1.37	$3^{1}/2$	3.20	$5^{1}/2$	5.03	$7^{1}/2$	6.86	$9^{1}/2$	8.69
$1^{5}/8$	1.49	$3^{5}/8$	3.31	$5^{5}/8$	5.14	$7^{5}/8$	6.97	$9^{5}/8$	8.80
$1^{3}/4$	1.60	$3^{3}/4$	3.43	$5^{3}/4$	5.26	$7^{3}/4$	7.09	$9^{3}/4$	8.92
$1^{7}/8$	1.71	$3^{7}/8$	3.54	$5^{7}/8$	5.37	$7^{7}/8$	7.20	$9^{7}/8$	9.03
2	1.83	4	3.66	6	5.49	8	7.32	10	9.14

index